FACE To FACE with Life

with Life

The Origin of the Peace Formula.

Face to Face with Life

What do the tragedies and trials of life mean to us? Are they to be seen as obstacles or barriers to our progress in life, or as significant and powerful markers of life leading us forward?

This is the true story of how tragedy became the catalyst for an inner explosion in the lives of two very different people.

Mansukh Patel, a young Indian boy growing up in the plains of the Rift Valley in Kenya, found himself exposed to the horrors of the Mau Mau uprising. John Jones, an English school boy from Middlesborough with a passion for football and climbing, experienced his young life being turned inside out by a tragic turn of events.

Neither of them had any control over the forces that were moulding their lives, nor could they have known that these seemingly cruel circumstances were to lead them on a unique journey together. Climbing on the back of a wave that seemed to have a power and momentum of its own they were brought together to explore the greater truth and purpose of their lives and to investigate the influences moving them. This friendship was to give rise to the Life Foundation which, as the Life Foundation School of Therapeutics, is today making its own waves across the world - waves that are changing people's lives and bringing hope and freedom to thousands.

Their story is astounding because it is true. It gives us all hope to be able to trust our life and to let go of the struggle that inhibits our ability to fulfil our highest dreams. It will make you laugh, it may make you cry, but it will definitely reach deep inside you and touch the part of you that is searching to know the truth.

Front and back cover design and photography by Regina Doerstel and
Jeff Cushing.

Front Photograph shows Dr Mansukh Patel entering the 1995 Life
International Conference at Bangor in North Wales after the Eurowalk
2000 journey from Auschwitz, having just received a garland of 1,000 Peace
Cranes from Japanese Buddhist monks participating in the Conference.

Back Photograph shows John Jones conducting interviews on Shankill
Road, Belfast during the 1995 Eurowalk through Northern Ireland and
Eire.

© Dr Mansukh Patel & John Jones 1996

First published in the United Kingdom in 1996 by
Life Foundation Publications
Maristowe House
Dover Street
Bilston
West Midlands WV14 6AL

Reprinted May 1998
Available in Dutch

ISBN 1 873606 10 9

Printed by Biddles Ltd, Woodbridge Park Estate, Woodbridge Road, Guildford
Cover and colour plates by R. Weston (Printers) Ltd, Dixon St, Wolverhampton

FACE TO FACE with LIFE

Pathways from Struggle to Freedom

Dr Mansukh Patel and John Jones

Compiled by
Sally Langford and Andrew Wells

Dedication

To our parents, who have been our teachers and guides for so many years and to all the great visionaries who have found truth. Mahatma Gandhi, Martin Luther King and Saint Francis and countless others have each found a part of the great whole and allowed it to flow through them to change the world.

Contents

Part four

Rebuilding Maristowe

Part five

Simple Living - High Thinking

Part six

Serving the World

Foreword

Looking all around me, I see at work in the universe a miraculous power that can take a tear and make it into a smile, hold a weakness in its hand and somehow make it strong. It is a power that can stand face to face with a fear and thereby turn it into an experience of love. This same sacred power lends us courage when on our own we have none. It heals our sense of separation and gives birth to creativity, levity, freedom and fun. The power that I speak of is the power of spiritual friendship and this book that you are about to read is a celebration of just that. Be prepared to be profoundly moved.

Never, ever underestimate the power of friendship for in truth, it is the power of love made manifest. The art of true spiritual friendship is to stand face to face with another and look beyond their fears, their past, their mistakes and see, really see, their spirit of love, which, just like a beautiful bird, longs to fly and to be free, to sing and to be heard. What you see is what you strengthen. What you give to another you gain for yourself. This is the miracle of friendship.

So, sit back and allow this beautiful book to inspire all of your friendships forever and take a moment to pray that you may be as generous a friend as Mansukh and John have been to one another. Isn't it wonderful how a simple, honest friendship such as they shared should become a platform for the Life Foundation - a worldwide living example of friendship without frontiers which has inspired thousands of people to live a more honest and more loving life.

One true act of joining is miracle enough to bless this world of ours forever. Let, therefore, your heart-felt call for love and for laughter melt your cold resistance to forgiveness, intimacy and freedom. And watch for the miracles that will surely follow. Truly, the greatest fun in life is to be the very best friend that you can be.

Robert Holden
Worldwide author, lecturer and broadcaster
on the healing power of love, laughter and an open heart.

Introduction

People are always asking us, 'How did the Life Foundation begin? How has it managed to grow from such a small beginning? What is it about your vision and dream that has inspired more than eighty people to give up all their time and energy to support your work for no financial reward?'

The Life family is a rich tapestry woven out of peoples' hopes and dreams for a better world. Many noble aspirations and high ideals form the threads but the canvas, the foundation, is made from their love, dedication and selfless service. I often wonder myself what makes these people so special and feel very grateful to have them in my life.

This is the story of the first decade of the Life Foundation, its origin, purpose and success. In this story we shall answer all these questions and many more, primarily to inspire others to believe in the incredible power of their own vision. The recipe for success in life is a relatively simple one and once known, it is a matter of acting skilfully and believing in one's ability to achieve the very highest in life.

The Life Foundation was originally conceived in the hearts and minds of two extraordinary people, affectionately known to us all as 'Mum and Dad.' They are the corner-stones of the Life Foundation and I have the privilege to call them my parents. Their vision and strength of spirit is, and always has been, the driving force behind all of our work. They were my teachers and guides throughout my life and it is through their wisdom and spiritual knowledge that I have arrived where I am today.

This is a miraculous story, and one that speaks to us all of the potential we each have as human beings. May it inspire you to reach for the very highest in your life.

Mansukh Patel

Chhaganbhai Patel

Echaben Patel

*'Transform the world by giving people
the tools to transform themselves.'*
Chhaganbhai Patel, 1975

Face to Face
With Life

My father and I were approaching the summit of Ben Nevis. The lush green wooded slopes of the glen had given way to a more rugged terrain as we climbed steadily through the morning. Even in July the moods of the Scottish Highlands are changeable and become inhospitable surprisingly quickly. As we neared the summit, cloud enveloped the bleak stony mountainside creating a cold, grey foreboding world.

For a fourteen year old on holiday it was an exciting challenge and, spurred on by the thought of the summit close by, I had pressed on ahead of the group. I was so exhilarated by the climb that I felt like shouting, singing and laughing all at once. Everything was so perfect.....

As I approached yet another hairpin turn in the path I heard someone call my name. 'John! Come quick!' a young woman shouted breathlessly as she struggled to catch up with me. Her face was anxious. Obviously something was wrong. 'Your father has fallen and he can't get up!' For a moment I hesitated, fearing what I was going to find, and then an invisible force seemed to take hold of my body as I almost hurled myself back down the steep path. A ghastly premonition was telling me something I didn't want to know. Fear gripped at my chest and numbed my mind.

My father was only forty nine and had always enjoyed good health. I could hardly remember him ever missing a day's work through illness. As an engineering surveyor he lived an active life back home on industrial Teesside. From a young age I had always been curious about his work-a-day world and as a special treat I had occasionally been allowed to accompany him on his visits to factories, iron foundries and steel rolling mills. As I ran down the path I could already sense that a big part of my life had just left me and that my childhood was about to end abruptly and decisively with a finality that would strip me naked.

As I reached him there was no trace of movement in his body and his lips were blue and lifeless. I couldn't bear to look, burying my face in his side as I hugged him in a desperate embrace. He was wearing the coat he wore for work to protect him against the cold of the mountainside. It had a familiar smell, a mixture of all the components of an engineer's life: oil, grease, machinery and hard work. It was the last time I would take comfort in that familiar smell. Another member of our party had been sitting by his side and I heard her telling a climber coming down the path that she was a nurse and that everything that could be done had been done and that someone had gone for help.

As the terrible reality began to dawn on my young mind I found myself half whispering, half crying, 'Don't let him die, please don't let him die.' At first the words just came automatically but then I began to pour my strength and feeling into them. Each time I repeated my prayer I reached deeper into myself, drawing on unexplored resources of strength. Then, quite suddenly and unexpectedly, I became aware of being heard. It was like a deep receptive silence, but at the same time came a sense that something much greater was being asked of me. I had a definite feeling that I had to give more of myself.

From the very depths of my being I found myself promising my life to serve the world and whatever greater purpose my Maker should give me.

It was such a natural outpouring that it brought almost a sense of relief and a feeling of coming home. What I didn't know then was that in my father's leaving he was giving me a precious gift, something he couldn't have given me in any other way.

*** *** ***

Less than four years later that prayer was to bring me into the life of an extraordinary man and a friendship that would take us both in a direction that would enable me to fulfil my promise....

Face to Face with Struggle and Freedom

———————————————— • ————————————————

There have been many times in my life when I, like John, have lifted my eyes to the heavens in a silent plea for meaning and purpose. Not least was the moment I held my father as he died in my arms, only a year after my mother's death. My parents were simple, indigenous people who had been my teachers and guides for over 35 years.

> **Life is a perfect dance between joy and pain**

Their own lives were full of turbulence, struggle and uncertainty, both in India and Kenya but, because they understood the spiritual and natural laws that govern the universe, they were able to look at every situation as a source of energy and potential for creating something greater. This attitude enabled them to learn from every experience so that they could use their knowledge to improve the lives of other people as well as their own.

Life is such a perfect dance between joy and pain that wherever we go and whatever we do we simply cannot escape this truth. Every one of us is seeking happiness and fulfilment, but if we can only accept the good

> **The tragedies and trials of life are there to take us towards our highest goal**

times and reject the difficult ones, we may find at the end of the day that we have missed almost half of our life.

It's a matter of understanding that the tragedies and trials of life are there to take us towards our highest goal, and not to deter us. I had to learn from a very early age to see every tragedy and encounter with life as perfect and in complete accordance with a divine plan. I was lucky to have been born into a deeply spiritual family to whom this knowledge came naturally.

On many occasions I found myself exposed to tragedy and pain, not only in my life but also in the lives of others. It was through this that I discovered the power of the truth my parents had imparted to me and the strength it had given me. Life can sometimes seem like a battlefield as we struggle against despair and doubt, against crises of anger, loneliness, sadness or fear. Yet deep within us all there lies a vast hidden reservoir of dormant potential just waiting to be called upon and utilised.

We are all standing on the mountain of life facing our own trials and tribulations every day. The question is, how do we respond to them? Do we move with the drama and rise above it to create something more meaningful or do we allow it to destroy us?

> **Deep within us all there lies a vast reservoir of strength**

We need to know what to do, how to think and respond to every circumstance. Armed with this knowledge we become invincible and able to use every situation as a stepping stone to higher things - no matter what has happened to us.

I was brought up in Kenya in a little town called Gilgil amidst the expansive plains of the Great Rift Valley. The valley has such a gentle feeling. It comes upon you slowly as the vast grasslands stretch out ahead of you and the thorn trees spread their shade over the plains. As a small child it seemed to me as though the world stretched away forever into the sunset.

But life in the valley was also hazardous and hair-raising, fraught with dangers from man and beast. Life was dangerous and uncertain not least because of the Mau Mau uprising. Many times I found myself witness to unspeakable horrors and atrocities that could easily have left me scarred for life had it not been for the indigenous wisdom that surrounded me.

Mansukh

The sun had just set and dusk enveloped the forest as my father walked briskly along, eager to get home, because he had just collected a month's wages and knew that the Mau Mau were very active in the area. As he reached the river and began to cross over the bridge he froze. There they were, right in front of him, fifteen to twenty fierce-looking guerrillas, each brandishing a long knife. Without hesitation he turned to go back, but there were more behind him. He was surrounded. Dad knew his time had come.

The Mau Mau were well known for their angry acts of violence and he knew he didn't stand a chance of survival. Something inside him surrendered to that. As they closed in on him he began to pray. What else could he do? He heard a voice demanding his money, and he quickly took out his wallet and threw it to them. He stood rooted to the spot, waiting for the inevitable, when suddenly a familiar voice said, 'Bwana? Is that you?' It was the voice of Kyoto, a young boy who used to come and do odd jobs for Dad in Nairobi where he worked. In return they often fed him and gave him clothes and even shelter.

'Kyoto?' Dad's voice was incredulous.

'Yes,' came the angry reply. 'What the hell are you doing here? Don't you know this is no place to be at night? Get out of here!'

This banter caused an animated exchange between the guerrillas who were all set to kill, and Kyoto who had a lot of affection and loyalty for Dad. In the end they reached a compromise and stripped him to his underwear, taking all his possessions and leaving him to walk home.

Meanwhile at home Mum had sensed that something wasn't right and lit a candle. I knew it wasn't time for prayers and was acutely aware of her concern. Feeling protective towards her, I curled into her lap and fell asleep while she prayed.

The next thing I remember I was being catapulted through the air, landing with a thud on the floor. Mum had heard footsteps on the veranda and in her anxiety had jumped up suddenly to greet my father, not realising I was there. The impact I felt from this was nothing compared to the shock of seeing the almost naked figure of my father standing in the doorway.

He was shaking violently from head to toe. My mother rushed over to him, wrapped her shawl around his shoulders and held him until his trembling stopped. They were both crying as they looked deeply into each other's eyes. I closed my eyes for I could hardly bear to feel their pain.

That night I slept very soundly, full of gratitude that my parents were still alive. The incident had completely changed my life. From that moment on I never again took it for granted that my father would always be there and I felt a great need to be with him more. After the uprising had died down he began, at my mother's suggestion, to take me with him wherever he went so that our relationship became much deeper and more meaningful for both of us.

I listened more intently to his teachings and participated more fully in being with him. My favourite treat was to have freshly-baked corn on the cob which was cooked by the side of the road and is the Kenyan equivalent of popcorn or French fries. Like the corn our relationship became golden.

*** *** ***

The drama of life is so real that it takes you right to the edge of questioning what is the most precious thing to you. Instead of using the situation to become sad, fearful or sorry for themselves, Mum and Dad used the power and energy of it to create something far greater. Although they had been totally involved in the drama as it unfolded they simply would not allow it to take them into a downward spiral.

The more traumatic an incident the more power it has.

The Search for
Happiness and
Success

Mansukh

Have you ever met someone for the first time and yet had the strangest feeling that you already knew them from somewhere? It was like this for me when I met John in the university refectory one morning. Amidst the noise and clatter of plates and cutlery and the hubbub of voices I was momentarily drawn into that strange sensation of déjà vu. He seemed to look at me a little warily but I was immediately struck by the kindness in his face. I could clearly see that here was a human being who was very compassionate and trustworthy. There was also something in his face that spoke to me beyond the words we exchanged and in his eyes the mark of the deepest pain was clearly visible. Something had happened to him that had changed him profoundly and left him questioning and searching for answers.

I felt compelled to find out what it was that had hurt him so deeply because I could feel a resonance between us. I knew he had touched something that I recognised, something almost intangible yet at the same time so real it was indelible.

As I got to know him we discovered we had quite a lot in common even though my subject was biochemistry and he was studying forestry. We both loved walking, sport and athletics and being anywhere in nature. I wasn't as keen on football as he was, preferring hockey and badminton, but he did his best to re-educate me.

Interestingly, he had an Indian girlfriend while mine was English, which we both found very amusing and which seemed to create a perfect balance somehow. I had a feeling that our meeting was a very significant landmark in my life although I could never have anticipated the depth of that significance.

John

I met Mansukh towards the end of my first year at university. My best friend Jas, who was a very sociable character, seemed to know everyone in the university and he told me about this interesting young Indian lad who did meditation and yoga. I remember feeling quite impressed and very glad someone was doing something like that although the whole idea of meditation was quite new to me. I found it interesting, but hardly anything that I would ever think of taking up. My life revolved around sport, which I loved, and a career in forestry, which was the only thing I had ever wanted to do.

Our first meeting took place across the breakfast table at our hall of residence. As we were introduced he looked at me with his penetrating eyes and smiled in a knowing kind of way. I had the distinct impression that he knew something about me that I didn't and this made me feel a little bit uncomfortable.

I soon found myself spending more and more time with Mansukh and the group of friends that were gathering around him. He was quite different from the average student, always buoyant and cheerful with a rare self-sufficiency and quiet confidence. Whilst he was always playful and ready to have fun, there was also a lot of self-discipline in his life. It was noticeable in the way he studied, his diet, his lifestyle, but most of all in the way that he spent time each day meditating.

I never suspected for a moment that this new friendship would have such a profound and far-reaching effect on my life, nor that it was to mark the beginning of a voyage of discovery that was to change and shape the rest of my life in a way I could never have imagined.

Bangor University is close to the sea and overlooked by the mountains of Snowdonia. Plas Gwyn, the hall of residence where we lived, is beautifully situated on an area of high ground in the university residential campus. The accommodation is built around three sides of a square, the fourth side being open and facing the mountains. In the centre of the building at that time was a well-kept lawn and around the borders were planted azaleas, rhododendrons and other flowering shrubs. A large sycamore tree grew in one corner of the square its spreading boughs giving the area a lush, leafy feeling.

Our rooms were situated in the most favourable position, facing the open end of the garden courtyard with the mountains only a few miles away in the distance. In springtime they were often capped with snow and, coupled with a blaze of red azaleas, provided a breathtaking view from our balconies. I often marvelled at the sheer beauty of our surroundings and the tranquillity which pervaded the building despite the often noisy inhabitants. It was an absolutely perfect setting for the adventure in living which our final year at university was to become.

Mansukh's room became famous in the university for two reasons. One was that is was an open house for anyone to come for tea, coffee and biscuits, and the other was that it was so tidy and calm. Compared to the often fraught and tense atmosphere of the university, you were immediately struck by the sense of stillness it radiated. This really fascinated me and I kept wondering how he did it.

There wasn't anything in his room that really reflected his cultural background. He had a lot of natural things like a swan's quill, a peacock feather, a shell and some rocks. A crystal hung from a thread at the window, catching the light and reflecting rainbow colours around the room. There was a beautifully carved wooden antelope which he called Socrates and quiet, evocative pictures on the walls. These pictures often became the subject of discussion due to their unusual classical symbolism.

The quietness of the room seemed to attract you even though it sometimes became like Piccadilly Circus. Mansukh had a kind of visitors' book which he asked people to sign and some days he counted over eighty signatures! He must have spent most of his grant on tea, coffee and biscuits.

Everyone knew he meditated twice a day because it was the only time he closed his door. A little sign went up which said, 'I am meditating. Please *do come back.' It made you feel welcome.*

Whenever I came in just after he'd finished I was always aware of a gentle feeling of calm in the room that made me wish I knew how to do it myself. I was becoming more than a little intrigued by his lifestyle and soon realised, as we all did, that his upbringing had provided him with some very powerful tools for coping with life.

What affected me most deeply was that he was always happy. I never once saw him depressed or sad, despite all the unhappy things that he had witnessed in his life. One morning we were walking together along the Menai Straits on the island of Anglesey and I asked him how he did it.

'You know, John,' he said, 'it's not as hard as people think. Happiness is our real nature.'

'Then why isn't everyone feeling happy?' I asked.

'Because they are looking in the wrong place. Our human predicament is just like the story of the musk deer my father used to tell me about.'

Y Garn from Llyn Ogwen

There is a deer that produces musk in its own body. At a certain time of the year the smell is released and the deer catches the scent on the wind. It becomes entranced, intoxicated and mesmerised by the exquisite aroma.

All it wants to do is to find the source of the perfume. It chases through the forest, seeking and searching until gradually it becomes more and more frantic because it never seems to get any closer to it.

It looks everywhere, in every possible place, never giving up hope until eventually it collapses, exhausted, at the end of the day. The next day it catches that smell on the wind and begins the search once again ....

The deer has no idea that the exquisite aroma it is so desperately pursuing is actually coming *from its own body* and that the very thing it spends its whole life seeking is lying right there within itself.

The Search for Happiness and Success

Happiness is not a distant goal, it is here - now!

Like the deer, we are all chasing something - in everything we do, in every place we go and in everyone we meet. Every day we set out on our search to find the source of happiness which we *know* is there, but somehow we just keep missing it. Momentarily we may touch upon it, thinking we have found it, but then it is gone again.

Inside us there is a feeling that if we keep moving and changing our experiences then sooner or later we'll find what we are looking for.

This is the greatest truth you will ever hear

Because we never do touch or grasp it, our search continues to extend further and wider all the time. So wide, in fact, that we completely forget to look in the most obvious place, which is *here*.

It's like looking for your nose. You could search the whole world but it's right there on your face! This confusion about what we are really looking for leads to a deep sense of disappointment and emptiness.

No-one will ever be able to tell you this truth unless they have stayed long enough in one place to taste it for themselves.

This is actually the greatest truth you will ever hear and maybe that is why it is so hard for us to believe that everything we ever wanted to feel is right here ... now ... inside us.

15

Pathways...

to Happiness and Success

◆ *Make a list of everything you need to be happy*
  * Look at each item in turn and ask yourself: 'How happy does this make me?' Decide whether this happiness is long-lasting, short-term or permanent.
  * Find someone you know who already has what is on your list and ask them if they are happy. Adjust your list!

◆ *Write down three things you love to do*
  Doing things that you love brings out the very best in you.
  * Schedule at least one of these activities into every day to help you to accomplish tasks that may not be so much fun.

◆ *What you focus on expands*
  Make sure you focus on success and happiness. Always spend ninety percent of your energy on solutions and only ten percent on problems.

◆ *What is your goal - and how will you get there?*
  Your destination can only be attained if you know what it is - and how to get there. Look at your list of things that you need to make you happy and ask yourself these questions:
  * Are they practical? Can I attain them?
  * What steps must I take now, next week, in three months and next year in order to reach them?

◆ *Take action - now!*
  Always start straight away. Think of something positive you can do, no matter how small, in order to start your journey towards your goal.

Ever since my father's death, questions would burn inside me which I never seemed able to answer. Meeting Mansukh was changing my whole perspective on life, giving me a sense of purpose that resonated with my innermost feelings and identity.

One Sunday as we were walking along the beach in the little town of Beaumaris on the island of Anglesey, I was reflecting on the transition that was occurring in my life. There were often times when I felt tired and stressed after long nights of study and encounters with people seemed to leave me agitated. At these times my mind would reflect on the words of this young Indian lad who was fast becoming a great friend. There was a peace and tranquillity about him that I longed for but never seemed to find and I knew instinctively that, intertwined with his experiences of the Rift Valley and the earth-born wisdom he'd learned there, lay the answers to my deepest questions. Luckily he never seemed to become tired of my incessant questioning.

Questions, so many questions. At last I had met someone I could sense was really listening, someone who could shed light upon my years of dimly lit wandering. I waited. As we walked my mind was bursting with thoughts, life images and decisions to be made.

'But what do we keep missing?' I must have looked very perplexed. 'Isn't it true that many things can make you feel happy? Surely we can't be missing it all the time?'

'Have you noticed the incredible colour of the water today?' he said. My mind suddenly became alive to just that - to the sun, the waves, the sound of our feet on the soft sand, the warmth of the breeze. Slowly I came to realise that my question had been answered. It was just a simple feeling.

Llyn Crafnant

A Simple Feeling

---•---

It is already inside us, there is nowhere to search

Most of us are looking for a feeling of joy and contentment. We often glimpse it in the magic moments of life. It may be a beautiful sunset that takes your breath away and reminds you of your timelessness, or those times when the stars are so vibrantly clear that you can feel the expansiveness of the whole universe.

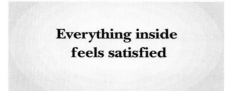

Everything inside feels satisfied

It could be the feeling you get when someone says, 'I love you,' or the exhilaration that comes from skiing at speed down a mountain slope.

You are totally absorbed in the moment, completely focused and not wanting anything else. Being in a state of total acceptance, everything inside you feels satisfied.

You will always know you've reached such a moment of contentment because you will find it so complete that there is nothing else you want. As soon as you find yourself wanting again - that's your signal that you've moved out of that feeling.

We all go to work so that life can have meaning, to try to fill ourselves up with that feeling of joy and love. But if we come back home exhausted, tired or angry at the end of the day, we will know that we haven't accomplished what we set out to do. We will then have to ask ourselves this: Why am I not feeling content?

We touch the greatest part of ourselves, a spark of our true nature

18

Whenever I listened to Mansukh I always had the same uncanny feeling that his words were almost going into me and satisfying something inside. It was like the sensation of drinking deeply when you are very thirsty. I know now that he was simply speaking the truth, but to me it felt as though his words were affecting me in a way I had been longing for all my life. Since my father died there had always been a part of me that was slightly numb and cut off from life. People say that something dies inside you when you lose someone you love and I did feel as though his death had left a huge void that nothing ever seemed to fill. It didn't matter what I did, it was always there.

In quiet moments I was aware of a kind of emptiness inside me, a hollow, aching space that cried out to be filled. I'd even got used to it being there and when it got too much I'd drink it away at the pub or do something exciting to distract myself. It never went away though, until I began to listen to the wisdom that to Mansukh was as natural as breathing. He'd been hearing it all his life from his parents and so it was a part of him but to me it was new, fresh and exciting and at the same time familiar. The strange thing about truth is that when you hear it for the first time, it sounds crystal-clear and obvious, as if you've always known it.

His words seemed to soothe and reassure me. The feeling that I had always wanted and had only ever touched briefly was right here inside me. It gave me hope and a thirst to learn more.

I asked him, 'What is it that stops us from experiencing that contentment?'

He answered simply, 'It's the wanting mind that keeps misdirecting us away from our centre. Remember the story of the deer?' He laughed softly.

The Experience of Wanting

—————————————————— • ——————————————————

Joy is not in things - it is in us

Our wanting mind never stops wanting! Every moment of the day it's giving out its commentary of wants and desires that will supposedly give us that feeling of happiness.

Have you noticed that whenever you get what you want another desire springs up almost straight away in its place? Our mind is insatiable in that respect. No matter what you get, achieve or

> **It is what Mother Teresa calls 'spiritual deprivation'**

accumulate it never says, 'Ah, now that is enough.' Instead it opens up new files with endless lists of things we simply *must* have in order to feel happy.

From early childhood our minds have been trained to externalise happiness. We try to find it in perfect relationships, exciting work, exhilarating holidays or magnificent food.

The only problem with desire is that it just breeds more and more desires which we can never really satisfy. Somehow though *we always think that it will.* This creates a deep sense of frustration within us because we feel certain that happiness exists within the desire and yet, just when we think we're close, it eludes us leaving us with a feeling of emptiness, confusion and loss.

This is what Mother Teresa calls 'spiritual deprivation', meaning that our spirit is deprived of finding what it is really looking for.

> **Desire breeds more desire**

'You know, John,' Mansukh carried on, 'desire is the most dominating and compelling force in human nature, but when misdirected it can destroy us. The whole of our society is geared towards fulfilling more and more desires, but eventually it can lead to our destruction.'

We had recently heard of the tragic case of four students from the university who had gone to a party one Friday night. Having had too much to drink, the driver lost control of the car and everyone was killed except him.

'Drinking and chasing excitement are portrayed as 'macho' things to do but this is a very sad example of what can happen when desire runs away with us. In trying to fulfil every desire we lose control of ourselves.'

I thought about those young people whose lives had so suddenly been taken. I, too, had experienced my fair share of pleasure seeking highs, too numerous to mention. I was feeling slightly uncomfortable. 'God, if he only knew the things I've done,' I thought. My mind was full of past images of parties, football pub crawls, morning hangovers, fast cars.

'Why do we feel such a strong impulse to fulfil desires?' I asked him.

'Desire actually comes from our innate hunger and longing to know ourselves or, more truthfully, to know God,' he explained.

◀ Eurowalk 2000 in Snowdonia, North Wales

The Experience of Desire

All desires create suffering

Any desire is an overwhelming longing to satisfy a deep need we feel we have. It is overwhelming in the sense that we find it hard or impossible to resist.

Every desire captures us in this way and is always accompanied by a total conviction that the fulfilment of it will bring us lasting happiness. It *can* bring us joy - but only for a moment as it soon wanes, leaving us searching for another possible source of contentment.

The force of desire directed inwards empowers real joy

A desire takes us out of being completely happy in this moment now. Desire is based on the belief that we are incomplete and need adding to. Satisfaction is a feeling of wholeness that exists already within us. It is not attainable externally and this is where we are all being tricked, time and time again. The wanting mind keeps telling us that the next time we'll find what we are looking for.

The force of desire directed inward to the real source of satisfaction empowers *real joy*. Directed outward, our real happiness becomes depleted.

The way out? Focus on what you *really* want.

When the perfectly controlled mind rests in the self only, free from longing for all objects of desires, then it is said, 'He is united.'
Bhagavad Gita

Pathways...

to Lasting Happiness

◆ *Focus on what you really want*
Look at the things you desire and ask yourself what you *really* hope to gain from them. For example:
* If you want a new car, are you hoping for freedom or perhaps respect from others?
* If you want a new house, you may actually be looking for security, comfort or proof you've achieved your goal in life.
* If you want love or a relationship, perhaps it's simply because you really want more self-esteem.

◆ *Distinguish between what you desire and what you really need*
Ask yourself:
* 'Will this desire give me freedom, or will it limit me and stop me from attaining what I really want?'
* 'What is essential and what is inessential in my life?' Inessentials often bring clutter which hinders us from reaching our real goals.

◆ *Now make a list of other ways you can attain your real goals*
For example, if one of your real goals is to have more freedom, your list might look like this:
* Take the kids for a walk on the beach.
* Go onto flexi-time at work.
* Hide my appointment diary for a week...
Write at least eight strategies per goal, and then enjoy yourself!
You'll have a great time putting them into practice.

Bosnian Grandmother, Eurowalk 2000

The Need for a Calm Clear Mind

I don't know if John was even aware that there was an intense hunger in his eyes. He was yearning to know something and to understand life deeply. He certainly didn't know how much his questions were affecting me and how they were drawing things out of me that I was naturally quite hesitant to share.

My life growing up in Kenya where the nomadic Masai wandered freely over the great plains of the Rift Valley was such a far cry from Bangor University and the mountains of North Wales. It always surprised me that people in Britain didn't seem to know the simple truths that my parents and the Masai had imparted to me and I quickly learned to hold what I knew very close to my heart as not many people in the West appeared to want to learn it.

But whenever I was in John's company I'd begin to feel his hunger pulling at my heart. I found myself saying and feeling things that meant a lot to me. And so it was that our friendship began to develop. He was awakening my need to share what I knew and I was somehow helping him to find answers to his questions.

It wasn't long before several other people were to be drawn into this avenue of mutual awakening. The first was a guy called Chris. I had often noticed him around the university because he wore the oldest blue duffel coat I had ever seen. It didn't appear to fit very well and he later explained that everything he wore always seemed to 'warp' after a couple of days. The duffel coat definitely fitted this description!

His hair grew endlessly past his shoulders and gave you the feeling it may never have been washed! I thought he looked very lonely and could really do with a friend.

There was something else about him that caught my attention. It went way beyond his appearance but I couldn't quite put my finger on it at first. I invited him to share a cup of tea with me in my room and soon realised that he was actually someone very special. He may have been scruffy, but there was a lot more to him than that. I invited him to join the group of friends that were beginning to meet in my room every evening but, once again, I never suspected that here was yet another person who was to play a major part in my future.

Mansukh

As a group of friends were beginning to gather around us we started to meet regularly in Mansukh's room in the evenings. Initially we came together as a group to share our individual thoughts, feelings and aspirations. In listening to each other we discovered a lot about our emotional and physical as well as spiritual states. I think Mansukh realised very quickly that the knowledge and wisdom his parents had imparted to him was not common knowledge. It became very apparent to us that we all had a lot to learn about things that were simply second nature to him. We all needed to learn to understand the spiritual laws that govern the universe. Although he never showed it, I think he may have been quietly shocked to discover that people in the West simply didn't know what to him were obvious truths.

The more we became aware of his deeply spiritual background, the more questions we had to ask him about his perception of reality. He would throw us all into confusion by saying things like, 'What are you going to do with your life?' or 'Do you anticipate reaching the age of forty with no answers for yourself or other people?' These were the kind of questions his father had asked him.

He told us that his father had always urged him not to waste his time. He had encouraged him to look carefully at the opportunity life was presenting to him and not to fritter it away on an empty material existence.

No-one had ever spoken to me like this before. Everything he said seemed to have such depth and meaning and echoed inside me for days afterwards. There was something in me that wanted desperately to understand what life was all about, something that needed to know that there was real purpose to being alive. I couldn't bear the thought of an empty existence that left me at the end of my life still wondering. By now I was completely hooked and every time I saw Mansukh I pestered him for more information. I was hungry for more words I could reflect upon, more pieces to the jigsaw that I called my life. He often shared the deepest truths that he had learned from his father and mother that were, I felt, so precious to him.

'But you know, John,' he would say, 'if you want to succeed academically or, in fact, at anything in life, you must develop a calm, clear mind.'

Calm Clear Mind

•

*A calm mind is one that is never disturbed
no matter what happens*

One of the most powerful discoveries to be made on earth is that no matter how much we have travelled or achieved or learned, the only way to really live a day without being caught up in the chaos of living is to cultivate a calm, clear mind. This state has been experienced by teachers from all the great traditions. In history we see that behind the lives of some of the greatest leaders like Mahatma Gandhi and Martin Luther King lies a life based around maintaining a calm mind.

Decisions made from a calm mind will always be the right ones

The confused and restless mind is like a monkey, jumping endlessly from one thought to the next. No matter what you do, it's always predicting, judging and thinking about what's happening next. Even when you are eating your dinner, it's wondering what's for pudding! Like a cat on a hot tin roof, it never stays in one spot for long, always chanting its endless mantra, 'what's next? what's next?'

We really need to know how to *defuse our restlessness*. But there is more to it than just controlling the mind. It involves cultivating an approach to life that gives us the perfect balance and poise to accept our life and *act in it* rather than *react to it*. The problem is that everyone is so busy these days rushing around trying to achieve so much. The Japanese alphabetical character for 'busy' literally translates as, 'to lose one's heart or one's centre' and this is *exactly* what happens when we go into the busy mode.

So much energy is wasted in rushing around but if we can just slow down, take it easy and focus our energy on staying calm, it is possible to achieve a lot more - and more efficiently.

28

P a t h w a y s ...

to a Calm Clear Mind

◆ *Stop rushing*
Take a moment out of your life to ground yourself. Whenever you find yourself rushing, stop and take four deep breaths.

◆ *The Heart-Power Technique ... de-stress in five minutes*
Next time you feel agitated or stressed take a moment for yourself.

* Breathe in deeply, pause, and as you breathe out, relax the key areas around your face, shoulders, hands, abdomen and thighs.

* Focus on the centre of your chest and feel the rising and falling of your sternum as you breathe easily and naturally. With each breath move your awareness deeper into your chest behind the sternum until you connect with your heart centre.

* Recall a totally positive, uplifting experience you have had in your life. Try to relive it as deeply as you can - make its image bigger, brighter, closer.

* Now, with this feeling, pause and take two deep breaths. Ask yourself what would be the best response to your situation to minimise future stress.

* Listen to what your intuition says and act on it.

With practice you will be able to use this technique at any time of the day to instantly diffuse stressful situations.

Great teachings, I thought, but a bit of a tall order amidst the tumult of university life that often left you feeling like a boat tossed on the waters of other people's thoughts and feelings. I felt as though I needed some kind of reassurance that I really could achieve such a high aspiration.

'It sounds great, but do you have any idea how hard it is to control the mind? I might just as well try to stop the wind.' I was feeling more than a little despondent.

'Hey, John,' he said lightly, 'do you feel like a walk up Snowdon? We can carry on our conversation while we are walking.'

As I looked at the early afternoon sun streaming through the windows I couldn't think of a nicer way to spend our time. We donned our walking boots and hit the mountain trail, but after about twenty minutes of walking my mind was still racing, full of questions about how to calm my mind. In fact, it was painfully obvious that I couldn't stop its feverish activity. I had to ask him, 'How do you do it then, Mansukh? How on earth do you calm the mind down?'

'The modern mind has become very agitated, John, through lack of discipline and focus and that is where meditation and silence can really help.'

'But what about people who aren't ready to meditate? Can they calm their minds down so that life doesn't become a stressful race to the grave?' I asked.

'You remind me of when I first came to this country,' he said. 'I was twelve years old and arrived in my khaki shorts to meet the bitter English snow. The biggest question I had after asking for snow to be explained to me was, 'Where's everyone rushing to?' I had never seen so many people going in so many directions, all at once, at such speed. Mum and Dad didn't know either!

'You must do things without rushing if you want to maintain a calm mind. People get so caught up in the paraphernalia of everything which makes us lose our strength, our joy and our splendour. We need to slow down enough so that we can become aware of our life. Mum always taught me to live each moment as fully as possible, almost making it 'tasty' and so nourishing that no two moments are the same.

'You know, there was a mountain near Gilgil my father used to take me to. We would sit there for hours together, just feeling the silence around us. I remember watching the gazelles gliding across the great plains and the

herds of zebra grazing in the long grass. People in the West need to take time to be silent because it offers a refuge where we can restore our energy and rest the mind.'

It sounded good to me and as we paused to rest on the old track I crouched down and closed my eyes. 'Might as well give it a try,' I thought. I took a deep breath and as a lone buzzard circled silently in the clear sky above us, I gave my mind permission to capture the vastness of the silence that surrounded us.

Waterfalls above Pinewood, Gerlan

Silence

———————————————— • ————————————————

Signals from the soul come silently

Have you ever really allowed yourself to become totally immersed in silence?

> **Silence is the language that goes beyond words**

Silence is the most precious gift we have. Although it is sometimes referred to as 'empty' it is actually full of riches, for it is from silence that *everything originates.*

If words are so powerful how much more so should be the silence that is the originator of those words. Mahatma Gandhi used to observe a day of silence every Monday and he once wrote, 'I started my weekly observance of a day of silence as a means of gaining time to look after my correspondence but now those twenty four hours have become a vital need.'

Deep and profound silence brings us into a state of balance that creates positive changes within and consequently all around us.

That strange guidance we call 'intuition', which is often pushed aside and neglected, is also born from the depths of silence. When we take time to sit quietly and let the mind settle down we can begin to hear the voice of our deepest nature, and with it comes a clarity about our purpose on this earth.

> **Silence is the most precious gift we have**

Pathways...

to Silence

◆ *Use your Environment*
Next time you are out for a walk pause for a moment and take a look at a bird in flight. Hold its presence in your awareness and capture its wings in flight. Then, as it disappears into the distance, close your eyes for a moment. Recreate that flight inside you and watch out for the explosion of meditative silence.

◆ *Listen to the Inner Sounds*
A quiet mind starts with a quiet body.
* Sit comfortably with both feet on the floor and back straight.
* As you breathe out relax your toes, calves, thighs, abdomen, chest, hands, arms, neck, face.
* Spend 4 minutes listening quietly to the ebb and flow of your breath and for the sound of your heart.

◆ *Still the Mind*
Choose something that helps you focus, such as a candle flame or a flower.
* Place it at eye level a few feet in front of you.
* Sit comfortably with your back straight, body relaxed.
* Breathe naturally and calmly.
* Focus on the object for 5 minutes. As thoughts come, let them wash over you without getting involved in them.

◆ *Make an Appointment with Yourself*
Take 5 or 10 minutes for yourself at the same time every day to practise any of the techniques from this chapter. You will create a deep reservoir of calm that you can draw from at any time.

The sun hung low in the sky as we began to walk down the old Miners' Track. In the depth of the silence the mountain offered, I felt excited by the power and strength I was touching. My mind had suddenly become crystal-clear, no longer cluttered by troubled thoughts. They seemed to have simply vanished, blown away like clouds on a windy day, leaving no trace behind them.

I felt charged and alive, exhilarated by the simplicity of my discovery. Being on the mountain had broadened my perspective considerably and I was able to see more clearly that there was an incredible force moving through my life. A pathway seemed to be opening up in front of me and all I had to do was follow it, moment by moment.

I was suddenly filled with an immense sense of gratitude to that power of life that refused to ignore the cry of my heart and was responding so readily to my longing to know the truth.

'My friend Rita came to visit me yesterday.' Mansukh's voice gently broke through my reverie.

'Oh?' I had only seen Rita a couple of times to say hello to, but I didn't really know her that well.

'She was talking to me about her anxiety problems. She feels a lot of pressure to succeed in her life and at the same time doesn't think she is achieving her best, which makes her feel very depressed a lot of the time.'

'What did you say to her?' I knew several people in a similar situation and was interested to know what Mansukh would offer as a solution.

'The first thing I suggested was that she should try not eating meat because I felt that would help her a lot. Then I talked to her about the power of meditation and offered a few simple techniques to start her off.'

'How did she respond to that?' I was curious.

'I think she was willing to try anything, but we'll have to see how she gets on.'

I had always associated meditation with the stillness I felt in Mansukh's room after he had been meditating. 'What is meditation exactly?' I asked. As I said it, I was sensing that once again life was about to take me yet one more step forward...

Meditation

●

Why not make the difference now?

Meditation helps us to break up the shell of inner resistance to our inherent contentment and shows us the way to properly orientate ourselves in life.

It is an indispensable tool to make sense of the chaos around us and the bitter disappointments and heart-breaking anguish of life. It is through meditation that we can really fulfil what seems to be the uncharted and unknown territory of our real self. It opens the door for us to see the truth of who we are.

Meditation is a clear and absolutely certain way to get where you really want to go instead of following a hit- and-miss journey in life.

Meditation is our deepest source of strength and power

It makes us face ourselves and is our deepest source of strength and power. Entering into it is like stepping into a still, cool lake on a hot summer's day. It soothes and refreshes - bringing such a great sense of relief. We emerge feeling invigorated and renewed, with a whole new inspirational perspective on everything.

If you have ever listened deeply to the dawn chorus, or sensed the silence of rapt attention in the theatre during your favourite play, you will know the feeling of meditation. It is the eternal joy of a thousand joy-filled memories all in one.

Meditation connects and gathers all the different parts of yourself so that you do not rush into the day feeling fragmented. It is a tool - a way to explore the reality of present life - and when practised regularly it can help us to maintain a state of perfect balance and a feeling of deep internal harmony. We could all do with this - couldn't we?

35

Pathways...

to Meditation

Meditation arises effortlessly when the body, breath, mind and emotions align with your heart. The secret lies in your preparation.

◆ *This is your time*
   * Find a clean, comfortable and inspiring place. It is where you recharge for the day so look after it well.
   * Make sure you won't be interrupted. It's OK to take the phone off the hook and to decide not to answer any doorbells.
   * Be consistent. Shorter periods at the same time each day will bring you better results than irregular bursts.

◆ *Effortless sitting*
   Posture has an enormous effect upon the way we think and feel.
   * Before you sit, ease stress and tension with a few simple stretches or a five minute walk. Try not to eat a heavy meal beforehand.
   * Sit with your back straight and erect. Use a chair or cushions to support your knees or pelvis so you can completely relax.
   * Imagine that a thread connected to the crown of your head is gently pulling you up.

◆ *The attitude for success*
   * Affirm 'I am now going to reach the highest part of myself,' and let nothing deter you.
   * Realise that you are taking this time for yourself so you have more to give to people.

Meditation to Renew Body, Heart and Mind

For a few quiet moments simply feel your breath flowing in and out. Then, as you breathe in, take your awareness to your feet and let tension ebb away from them as you breathe out. With each new breath relax your calves, thighs, pelvis, abdomen, chest and back. Let your hands and arms become heavy and relax your shoulders, neck and face. Let each outbreath soothe away stresses and blockages. Your body feels lighter now, like a friend.

Let the colour blue begin to permeate your body like a soft mist. Be aware that your emotions are present in this blue mist. Gather the molecules of the mist together and gently allow them to solidify. Affirm to yourself: 'My emotions are becoming still. I am free to be myself.' Feel how beautiful it is to simply sit, still and calm.

Think now of a fountain of golden light, pouring down through the crown of your head, flowing through you and slowly replacing all of the blue. Fill yourself with this soft golden light, allowing it to permeate every cell in your body. Let yourself become completely golden, silent and at peace. For a few moments listen quietly to the silence without needing to hear anything at all.

Let an inner smile of complete calm and peace emerge from the silence. Let your smile lightly touch your lips and flow down to your hands and palms. Move your fingers gently, and slowly open your eyes.

'It was the Masai who really taught me the power of meditation,' Mansukh said.

We had slowed down our walking pace and now both of us turned to look back across Lake Glaslyn. A crescent moon was clearly visible in the evening sky reflecting the quiet of the mountain.

'Tell me what it was like to be with them,' I said.

In the half light his face seemed to take on a quiet depth as he thought back to his childhood.

'They are such a majestic people,' he said, 'and as truly an expression of Africa to me as the immense scenery of the Rift Valley, the giraffe, lions and buffalo, the acacia trees and extinct volcanoes.' His voice was full of feeling as he spoke.

'They are nomadic wanderers who change their abode according to the season, the rains and the grazing. They are tall, dark-skinned and silent in their ways and carry themselves erect, chins stretched forward, as proud as statues.

'I felt such an empathy with them - and a real sense of oneness. They held a fascination for me so that something deep within me resonated with their lifestyle and philosophy. I spent almost all my time with them learning their ways and watching how they lived.

'They are the most natural of people and so free. They exude a strength and power of fearlessness which I believe comes from their knowledge of the earth. They know they are a part of her, just as the grasslands know and the animals and insects know. Their existence is in perfect harmony with their environment, and consequently Mother Nature has rewarded them with a wealth, seldom known or even equalled by any other primitive people.'

'What did they teach you, Mansukh?' I was really curious.

'That there is a way of living with integrity and dignity,' he said quietly. 'Because they understood the importance of the ancient ways and would never compromise their cultural values, they stood as a race apart and to this day still hold to the sacred laws.

'To me they were a living culture and my only education at that time. There was something about them that made me love to be with them. Although they were war-like in their ways there was a gentleness and a depth of wisdom I could sense in them.

'So often I remember sitting in the long grass as a small boy amid the

Masai

grazing Masai cattle, the herdsman standing noble and firm, motionless beside me. He would stand for hours on one leg, the other leg bent at the knee and resting just above his other knee, almost like a yogic Tree posture. This was their contemplative mode, and if you were wise you would never disturb them when they were standing like this. I would just sit and listen with them, feeling the depth of their silence and the stillness that enabled them to stand like this for hours on end.

'They taught me to listen to the wind and the cry of the eagle, to watch for the signals and signs that were all around. I learned to listen to the universe through stillness and observation, watching, feeling - and how to interpret those signals. I discovered that there is a symphony playing all the time in the elemental dance and each living thing is a part of it. Every sound, every movement is significant to the Masai and tells its own story.'

As he spoke I could almost see the little Indian boy running through the long grass of the great plains, so vibrant and free, so excited to be alive. For the first time it struck me how strange it must be for him to be here in this culture that seemed so divorced from nature.

'Do you miss living in Kenya, Mansukh?' It seemed a natural question to ask.

'I love being wherever I am, John.' He smiled. 'Everywhere has its own magic. Look at this, for instance.' He stretched out his arms to indicate the panorama of Snowdonia's peaks and laughed, slapping me on the back as we both turned to go down. 'We'd better get back,' he said.

Snowdon Massif from Capel Curig

As the term unfolded, we began to learn how to meditate. We would meditate on our own in the mornings and evenings but decided to sit together every Sunday before lunch.

'What's the best colour to meditate in?' I asked.

'Orange has always been associated with a contemplative life in my tradition,' Mansukh replied.

My hopes fell. I could see that it was going to be a very difficult task to find orange clothes as none of the group wore that colour neither did student grants stretch to buying new clothes.

One Sunday morning as everyone gathered for our usual session of meditation I burst through the door feeling triumphant. 'Look what I've got!' I said holding up a pair of bright orange workman's dungarees that appeared to be several feet wide.

Everyone stared at me blankly, waiting for an explanation.

'This is it, folks! Our meditation gear!' And I pulled out several more pairs with matching T shirts. Everybody groaned. The dungarees were so outrageous, however, that everyone had to put them on and there we sat, straight backed and alert in our voluminous fluorescent orange trousers looking like a row of giant carrots!

'Good job we keep our eyes closed is all I can say,' said Chris who was renowned for his dry sense of humour. 'We'll soon get used to them,' I said reassuringly. Sure enough, after a few weeks of wearing them someone suggested that if we were really serious we shouldn't be afraid to go down to lunch with them on.

'Why?' I asked feeling very nervous at the thought of it.

'Why not?' Everyone agreed that we should make a stand for what we believed in and so we marched into the refectory parading our matching bib 'n brace sets, completely oblivious to the gasps of admiration from over a hundred and sixty disbelieving faces. Actually, if the truth be known, we were pretty scared and it took a lot of guts. We soon became known as 'The Orange Brigade'.

Sunday morning became our regular appointment for 'satsang' and meditation. 'Satsang' is a Sanskrit word meaning ' the company of truth'. It was during these times that I felt the deepest bonding took place between us all because we were sharing something that was profound and new. Some of the discussions afterwards were so powerful that they effected very deep changes in us. In fact, the whole quality of our lives was beginning to change quite dramatically. There were obvious changes like giving up meat and alcohol, but accompanying these new facets of our lives were many more subtle shifts in our attitudes and perceptions.

Losing my father had made me realise how important relationships were in my life and as the weeks went by I could feel my heart and mind opening to the people around me. We were sharing our inner feelings and most private thoughts, helping each other to awaken to what we really wanted from life. Taking shelter within ourselves we were somehow becoming innocent again.

Slowly and surely we found ourselves entering a new and exciting dimension that was profound and also, you could say, surprising. We all felt as if something was driving us to explore a whole new reality. It was like being in a boat that was just pulling us forward towards an unknown destination. The friendship between us all had now become much more than just social acquaintance. The way we related to each other was deepening all the time, supporting and stimulating the process of inner discovery we were each experiencing.

Initially our individual role had been that of students, but gradually as we shared more of our spirituality we began to experience a massive paradigm shift. It was almost as though we were moving out of a left brain mode of experiencing life and into a space where a higher intuition was taking over, providing us with increasingly deeper and more profound insights.

It was during our finals that I could really see the effect of our meetings and meditation practice. The atmosphere in the university at that time was very intense, reflecting the way everyone was feeling. Our fellow students seemed to be all suffering from mental and emotional exhaustion and stress levels were reaching untold heights. Meditation was definitely working for us, however, because we only seemed to be experiencing a sense of 'mild apprehension' around our exams.

By now our perspective on life had altered so much that, although finals meant a lot to us, they definitely were not the most important thing any more. Life had become a much richer experience and everything seemed to be tinged with depth and meaning. It was almost as though we had stepped through the back of a wardrobe into another world, just like in the storybook. Everyone just sailed through.

We needed a name to bond and hold our group together so we decided to call ourselves 'The Life' and started looking for a symbol to go with it. Someone had found a picture of Duhrer's 'praying hands' and told us the story behind it. Looking at Duhrer's drawing I was suddenly struck by the power of those hands and their symbolism. I wanted to understand their significance more deeply so I turned to Mansukh and asked, 'How do you pray?'

He closed his eyes, put his hands together and said nothing for what seemed like a very long time. A stillness came into the room that compelled us all to close our eyes to sense it. I don't know what anyone else felt but to me it was one of the deepest moments in my life. It felt as though something moved inside me, as if my heart was bursting with an exquisite pain. Tears rolled down my face as I sat quietly feeling the depth of his prayer. When I opened my eyes I knew that we had all been changed in some way, and a pathway had been carved through our togetherness.

'That's our symbol,' someone said, echoing all our thoughts. Mansukh took out a little statue of the praying hands that he had found in Bilston market the week before when he was visiting his parents.

'Here's a co-incidence,' he smiled. 'Life is like that. It is always leading us on, giving signals and clues to indicate which way to go next. To me, spirituality is about developing such a personal relationship with the divine, that we are constantly aware of the guidance it offers. The praying hands will symbolise our commitment to that relationship and to serving others.'

Someone had also come across the Serenity Prayer and when they read it out we all felt it contained a message for us. That weekend Chris found some medallions in Guildford Cathedral with the praying hands symbol on one side and the Serenity Prayer on the other. Another coincidence? Something was going to a lot of trouble to put signs and signals in front of us and because we were picking them up life was nothing short of magical. One thing after another seemed to be happening to make it very clear to us which way we should go. Little did we know, however, just how perfectly the praying hands epitomised the work we would be doing in the future.

The Praying Hands

Albrecht Duhrer and his brother were both gifted artists, but as there wasn't enough money in their family to even support one of them at Art School, the two brothers decided to help each other to achieve their dream. Their plan was that one of them should work to support the other at school, and then they would change roles later on.

So it was that Albrecht went to study art while his brother worked in a factory to earn the money to support him. After five years, he came home to fulfil their agreement and to give his brother the same opportunity. To his horror he discovered that his brother's hands were so damaged from his labours that he was no longer able to draw or paint.

Never once had his brother complained or even spoken about the hardship of his work and Albrecht was deeply affected by his sacrifice.

He drew his brother's hands to immortalise the memory of his selflessness and the image he created was to become synonymous with prayer and sacrifice throughout the world.

God, grant me the serenity
To accept the things I cannot change,
The courage to change the things I can,
And the wisdom to know the difference.

Something was really beginning to happen to me, almost as though a part of me was waking up for the first time. One morning after finishing my meditation practice I went onto the balcony of my room. It was a bright, sunny spring morning and the air was fresh and fragrant. As I looked across the courtyard I began to see what looked like swirling currents of mist in the air and around the trees and plants. I looked away momentarily to see if the bright sunlight was playing tricks on my eyes but when I looked again there they were. The same swirling currents of mist.

Later that day I told Mansukh about the experience. He explained that because of our new diets and practices we were becoming more sensitive to the subtle energy which permeates and vivifies the world of gross matter. Whilst new perceptions of this kind were interesting, far more beautiful was our awakening to the love, peace and beauty that lay within us and within others. At times, especially after having meditated, I would experience people in a dramatically new way. I became aware that the body was just a shell, a vehicle for the essence of what a person really is. And that essence, even though the person is not aware of it, is divine, effulgent and untarnishable. Sometimes, just by looking at people, I could sense how awake they were to their real nature. I was able to sense an almost visible denseness to people who were asleep to their essence whilst others, living more in sympathy with their real nature, were light and vital.

I remember being in such a heightened state of awareness when I met Mansukh's father and looked into his eyes. Who he was filled his whole frame. There was nothing else there. He knew I was really seeing him and just smiled gently and knowingly.

I was beginning to feel a great sense of urgency. We were all due to graduate in the summer of '78. Our respective careers were already taking shape and I had been offered a job in Nepal for three years on a forestry project. There was a possibility that what we had been building between us could be washed away as the world's currents picked us up and scattered us around the globe.

I felt that we had to somehow create a foundation so solid and firm that together we could build the future on it - a future based on our highest aspirations of serving life's essence. As our final exams approached my practice intensified as I reached out to grasp the opportunity that life was presenting us with.

The Upward Force of Life

———————————•———————————

The power of life itself

Our life is a constant interplay between two vital forces.

The first force comes from deep, deep within and is the power of life itself. It is the impulse that invites us to grow, to expand and to touch the heights of life. It calls out to us in the mighty strength of the redwood trees, in the majesty of high mountains, in the high drama of waves crashing against a cliff, in the glory of a mother giving birth to her child.

It awakens inside us when we hear of great acts of heroism, when people risk their lives to save others, face to face with life's great drama.

> **The interface between these two forces is the drama of life**

This force kindles our yearning for happiness and success and its end-point is that special feeling of attainment we all yearn for but can never quite put into words. This force of life, that lies deep within us all, is the upsurge of our true nature longing to express itself.

The second force might be called the downward inertia of disbelief that first started when someone told us we were not good enough or that we definitely couldn't achieve our goal. These beliefs have been reinforced ever since by parents, friends, colleagues, advertising and finally by ourselves.

This second force only exists because of our belief in what we have been told. Every goal we've missed, every time we've failed, every heart-break and broken dream we've ever suffered has occurred because at some deep and hidden level we have believed in the voices of limitation.

47

'What are we going to do now?' Chris was voicing all our thoughts. 'We can't just split up and go our separate ways.'

Our finals were over and it was time to leave university, but none of us could bear to lose our new-found spirituality. We also knew that we wouldn't be able to tap into this magic on our own, without each other's help.

'Let's hire a big Luton van.' I suggested. 'We've got to get all our stuff back home anyway, and then we could stay in the van until we find a place to be together.' And that is exactly what we did.

The inside of the van looked like Aladdin's cave by the time we had neatly draped all our possessions over every possible corner, nook and cranny. We even had a little table with Chris's rubber plant. It was so large that we used to call it 'man eater!' We drove around the country for a while dropping off each other's stuff at various parental homes and simply enjoyed being together.

We ended up staying in a flat in London that belonged to Mansukh's sister, Savita. This became our home for the rest of the summer and everyone managed to get odd jobs around London to make ends meet. I got a job working for the council as a gardener while Mansukh worked in the design department of a Frisbee factory where he immediately caused a stir by doing yoga on the grass outside during breaks. His graceful flowing movements captivated so much attention that soon he had almost half of the entire staff joining in, including the manager!

In the evenings we all came together to eat and share our different experiences of the day and to sing and share satsang late into the night. As we fell asleep Chris always sang 'Stairway to Heaven' or 'Bridge over troubled Water', songs that will always remind me of those carefree summer days of '78. It was an extraordinary time for us - a time of delving deep into living truths, exploring and expanding the reality of our lives.

We were beginning to understand ourselves and to become more absorbed into our inner nature. Dad was there that summer and he was great to have around because in his presence I always felt safe. He inspired that feeling of complete confidence that somehow makes you feel very secure and his wisdom guided us all deeper towards taking shelter within ourselves. There was a childlike quality about our thirst to absorb the knowledge that was being offered to us as we realised more and more that what we were inside was infinitely more important than what we were doing.

I asked Dad whether he thought I should go to Nepal or stay with the group. 'No problem,' he said. 'Come and see me tomorrow morning, three thirty.'

Dad would never help you unless you first made an effort to find out and, quite honestly, getting up that early was an effort! I dutifully woke up and found Dad sitting cross-legged on the kitchen floor, his grey shawl wrapped around him. He took a couple of sips of the tea I offered him and then closed his eyes and was silent. I waited for ages, not knowing if I should repeat my question or keep quiet. The atmosphere was quite amazingly calm, as it always was around him, and I didn't want to disturb it but eventually I said, 'What's the best thing to do, Dad? Should I go to Nepal or stay here?'

He just said, 'Very simple, no problem.' And that was it!

It was obvious that our meeting had come to an end and as I didn't appear to be any the wiser, I just accepted that this was how it was.

Later in the day, however, I became aware that what had been a great conflict and a really difficult decision to make had suddenly become crystal clear and it was now obvious to me that the thing to do was to stay and not go to Nepal.

In some mysterious way Dad had precipitated this realisation in my mind that morning and this gave me an even deeper insight into the power of his silence and how very deep it was.

Summer ended and Mansukh went back to Bangor to do his Ph.D. while Chris stayed on at his teaching job in Hampstead and everyone else got jobs in different places. We agreed to meet at Mum and Dad's, in Bilston, every third weekend. Those weekends were designed to keep us going for the rest of the month and as soon as we arrived on Friday we started our meeting, which lasted until Sunday afternoon when we stopped to eat. We hardly slept or ate for the whole weekend, but just sat together singing and sharing the truth. Every time we shared what was meaningful to us it seemed to change the quality of our lives somehow. Those were magical times for us.

We didn't even notice the time going because we were so intoxicated by the atmosphere. Mum and Dad sat with us and taught us how to sing Indian 'bhajans', traditional songs from their homeland, of which Mum knew over five hundred. When they sang together it was as if they transported us to another age. I often wondered how two old indigenous

people, singing their hearts out, could have such a profound effect on us.
We never seemed to get tired of singing, in fact it seemed to energise us
more than anything else and the only time we stopped was to listen to Dad's
discourses. He knew exactly when to add his energy to the gathering. He
would start to speak, sometimes in his broken English but more often in his
own language while Mansukh translated. This was the highlight of the
weekend because he was such a wise man and his spiritual power was
immense and tangible. When he spoke it was as if his ancient lineage was
speaking to us. Many nights we sat spell-bound by his presence, captivated by
the words he spoke, as if transported to another world. Often the birds woke
up before we had gone to sleep; everything had become timeless. After a
while none of us could tell if it was day or night because we were oblivious to
everything but the magic of the moment.

T. Patel

What is the best time to do each thing?

Now - the only time you have at your command.

Who is the most important person to be with?

The person in front of you.

What is the most important thing to do?

To bring happiness to the person you are with.

My Relationship with Myself

It felt so good to be back home again. As soon as I walked in the door of our tiny terraced house in Bilston the atmosphere enveloped me in its welcoming embrace. The familiar smell of Mum's cooking and the sound of Indian music drew me back into their world and the land of my roots.

As I greeted Mum and Dad in Gujerati I was reminded once again of how comfortable one's mother tongue is and of how much I loved it. I picked my mother up off her feet and swung her around and she hit me on the back with her fists like she always did, pretending not to like it. I knew they were pleased to see me too and we sat down straight away to catch up on our news. As I listened to Dad, Mum sat on the floor, separating lentils one by one, silently participating in our togetherness. I was struck, as I have been so many times, by how much they meant to me and what strong anchors they were in my life.

'So what's happening for you now, Manu?' Dad said. 'How's the meditation group getting along?'

'Well,' I beamed at him, 'to be honest, Dad, it's been developing much more rapidly than I ever expected. As you know from the last time you came and spoke to us, the atmosphere is always electric when we are together, in the same way it is when you and I meet. They are hungry for your teachings and the knowledge you have given me.' Dad's face was expressionless as he listened, giving no indication of how he felt about it. 'I think everyone is reaching a point where the path of truth and living a spiritual life is becoming the most important thing. Things are really beginning to work for them and the group is gelling in such a way that no-one wants to separate at the end of term. In fact we seem to be moving towards a communal life.'

Suddenly Dad's eyes became very bright. 'Is that what you want to do, Manu?' he asked.

'That's why I'm here, Dad,' I said. 'I need to know whether I should continue to share what I know with them or to move on in another direction.'

Dad's eyes were glittering with excitement as he said, 'You know, what is happening in your little group has a great potential for the future.' His small body seemed charged with electricity. 'It reminds me of the time I spent with Gandhi and how committed we were to living the teachings and putting them into action. Gandhi always said, 'A small body of determined spirits fired by an unquenchable faith in their mission can alter the course of history.' From what I've seen of the group, they seem to have the same kind of strength and commitment. With proper guidance, who knows where it may lead you.'

'But is that the direction I should go in, Dad?' I wanted to be very sure.

'As long as your intention is to serve others and to share the teachings with as much discrimination as possible. You know that up until now the teachings have only ever been given by word of mouth. The time is different now. People need to know. You can transform the world by giving people the tools to transform themselves.

'Still, the choice is yours, Manu. You can go on alone or you can walk into the future as a group. The first option is much easier for you, believe me. In fact, you'd be crazy to carry on!'

He smiled because he knew and I knew that I could not resist his challenge.

When I left them on Sunday evening to go back to Bangor, I felt strong and clear once again. No matter what was involved in staying together, I knew we could do it.

Mansukh

Mansukh, Mum and Dad

My girlfriend and I had always been very close. Jas introduced me to her one day as we were walking up Glanrafon Hill and I remember looking at her and thinking, 'There is someone I could really love.' I thought she was beautiful. We became involved in the group together and I had always thought she felt the same way about it as I did. But things were becoming very strained between us as she sensed my increasing absorption into my spirituality. I felt so strong and full within myself these days that I no longer had the same kind of emotional needs and this seemed to be causing her a lot of pain, almost as though she needed me to need her.

'What can I do?' I said to Mansukh. 'I still love her and want to be with her, but I want her to share my inner awakening. I want her to feel the way I feel.' As I heard the words I was speaking I realised that it could never be that way.

'It's a strange thing that happens in relationships,' I explained, 'that whenever one partner is feeling stronger, the other seems to become even weaker somehow. I don't really know why or what to do about it.'

'One of you needs to let go,' he said gently. 'When you love someone and let them go their own way they'll come back if they are meant to, because essentially you are allowing the universe to guide you. But if you keep pushing and pulling it only creates more pain.'

As he spoke my mind flashed back to the last time I had been with her. We had walked across the campus together and then she had turned away to go to her lecture while I began to walk up to my room. For some reason, I had stopped and looked back. I watched her as she walked away and something inside me said, 'She has to go her own way.' It was such a painful thought that I immediately shut it out, but Mansukh's words brought it back to me with a crystal clarity.

'Everyone has their own path to follow in life, John, and we can always choose to struggle against the flow of what is meant to be. But in the end we will have to go with it.'

I could feel the pain of struggling against the situation. We were moving in different directions and there was nothing either of us could do to make it happen the way we would like it to.

I had to let her go.

The Nature of Struggle

•

'I believe that not a leaf moves but by God's will.'
M.K. Gandhi

Why do we struggle so much in life? Why doesn't everything run smoothly and just the way we want it to?

Everything in creation from the smallest molecule to the greatest planets is flowing effortlessly because there is an immaculate perfection about the way the universe works.

Think about anything in nature - the way the oceans ebb and flow in a perfect dance with the moon's magnetic influence, the way the birds start to sing in the morning as soon as

Struggle is our own creation

the sun begins to rise. And what about the way the sun rises and sets, setting fire to the sky, just it seems, for our delight? Absolutely everything is moving and flowing in perfect harmony with everything else - except for us!

We have chosen to interfere with this grand scheme of perfection and create a new phenomenon we call 'struggle'. We highly evolved human beings have powerful opinions about what should or should not happen to us and this leads us to interfere with the natural flow of things to try to *make* things happen.

In our search for inner and outer harmony the only place to start is with ourselves

The depth and magnitude of our struggle in life is directly related to the way we relate to ourselves.

A harmonious relationship will be reflected in the events and circumstances we attract to us. In our search for inner and outer harmony the only place to start is with ourselves.

We persuaded Chris to leave his teaching job in London so that he could move up to Bangor to live with us all in Pant-y-Lon, our little rented miners' cottage in the Welsh hills. Mansukh had begun teaching yoga in the university and more than a hundred and twenty people were turning up every week. I think he realised that because Chris didn't have a job he was feeling a bit lost, so he asked him to help to teach his yoga class.

'But I don't know any yoga.' Chris looked alarmed.

'Better learn quickly then.' And Mansukh left him with it.

Chris was like a fish out of water, floundering wildly in the belief that what he was being asked to do was completely impossible. But Mansukh would counteract his doubts with favourite phrases from his father. His favourite one was 'Everything is possible to the one who believes in himself.'

'Yes, but...' Chris was confronted.

'Believe in yourself, Chris. You are unlimited and able to achieve anything.' Another of Dad's quotes.

As he battled with inadequacy Mansukh took him through some basic movements and then put him in front of the class the following week. He carried it off beautifully. I asked him later why he had made Chris do it.

'Sometimes we need to be pushed to discover what we are capable of achieving,' he said. 'Dad always warned me not to become locked within my own self-imposed limitations. By leaving his job Chris has propelled himself out of the mental comfort zone and into a place where his self worth is in question. This is because we so easily fall into the trap of believing that our value is measured by what we do or what we know. That is why Chris's position is a very powerful one, spiritually speaking, as long as he chooses to see it that way. It is a time to really explore beyond the boundaries of who he thinks and believes he is and to test the truth of what we have been experiencing and feeling to be the highest truth during our years as a group.

'It's all very well sitting around together and talking about our true nature but it really has to become a practical and a living experience for us.'

My Relationship with Myself

There is no need to create a new you,
the you now is totally adequate

The greatest challenge we seem to face is thinking that we are not adequate. It is programmed into us from birth to always strive to be 'more' or 'better' than we already are, and to become 'somebody'.

The great Indian scripture, the Bhagavad Gita, beautifully portrays this human predicament in the character of the great warrior Arjuna.

Each one of us is on the battlefield of our life, facing ourselves every day

On the battlefield Arjuna becomes overwhelmed by despondency because he feels completely inadequate to do what is being asked of him. Krishna, his charioteer, has to convince him that he is indeed a great warrior and an unlimited being, capable of anything he sets his mind to. It takes Krishna the whole of the Gita to do it and only then is Arjuna able to fight.

Each one of us is on the battlefield of our life, facing ourselves every day, and the feelings that betray our greatness. Do not worry if you find that your opinion of yourself is not so high. It seems to be a part of being human and the art is to learn habits of thought that help rather than hinder us. Very few people have a truly high opinion of themselves and those that do have had to work very hard at it!

Until each one of us, like Arjuna, can discover our innate greatness, deep down we will always feel inadequate. This deep rooted belief forces us to build up an armoury of achievements to 'prove' we are great. We strive to get a good job, lovely house, financial security etc. The only flaw in this plan is that if any one of them goes our sense of self worth goes with it.

59

Pathways ...

to Complete Adequacy

◆ *How to think highly of yourself*
  * Think about everything you have been exposed to
    in your life and congratulate yourself on how far you have come.
  * Forgive yourself for not being what you think you should be.
    Change never happens through feeling guilty.
  * Build your self-worth on your successes and think about apparent
    failures as stepping stones for improving yourself. Successful
    people *learn* from their mistakes.
  * Separate yourself from your skills. It is important not to judge
    yourself by what you can or cannot do.

◆ *Jump in!*
  Always jump in at every opportunity. Rather than holding back say,
  'Yes! I can!' to yourself whenever a challenge arises.

◆ *Experiencing unconditional adequacy*
  Adequacy comes from really knowing that you are already whole and
  complete. Use the Heart-Power Technique on page 29.
  * Work through the technique until you feel calm and positive.
  * Visualise some of the highest moments of your life. Relive them
    as vividly as you can, letting the exhilaration of those moments
    flood through you.
  * Affirm to yourself: 'I am completely adequate.'
    Repeat your affirmation at least five times.
  * Let the feeling of complete adequacy fill your body and mind.

◆ *Affirm*
  Remind yourself who you really are by using affirmations constantly.
  In certain cultures chanting is used to evoke the very highest within
  a person. (See page 83)

Chris   Sir George Trevelyan

P a t h w a y s ...

to Loving Myself

◆ *How do you feel about yourself?*
  * Do you get on or are you always in conflict? If we cannot be a best friend to ourselves then who else will be?
  * Do you look in the mirror and think, 'You're the best!' or 'Oh no! Is that really me?' If someone compliments you do you cringe or fully agree?

◆ *How do you talk to yourself?*
  Be aware of your internal dialogue. Do you speak kindly to yourself or do you find you are self-critical and impatient with your limitations? Can you imagine being as gentle and kind to yourself as you would be to someone you love very dearly? Condemning yourself only empowers imperfections, which doesn't help at all.

◆ *Begin by accepting yourself as you are now*
  Self acceptance gives us a solid platform from which we can make real and lasting changes. You simply cannot wait until you have become what you think you should be.

◆ *Self love begins at home*
  * Nurture your body - with vital food, regular exercise, deep breathing and an upright and relaxed posture.
  * Create a supportive environment with pictures and colours that inspire you. Include plants and as much natural light as you can in your home and choose music, TV programmes and reading material that uplift rather than depress you. If you have to watch the news never eat at the same time.

Mansukh always saw every situation as positive, no matter how it appeared. To me, Chris really seemed to be struggling with himself in a way that I hadn't seen him do since we first met him at university. Mansukh saw it differently and to him Chris was on the edge of a great breakthrough.

As we sat round the fire one evening in the little sitting room at Pant-y-Lon, Mansukh began to talk about his mother.

'You know, Mum never learned to read or write. To the western way of thinking she is completely uneducated, although to me she is the wisest woman on earth. She knows everything there is to know that really matters even though she has never even read a book in her life.'

I was suddenly struck by the fact that here was Mansukh, studying for his doctorate in cancer toxicology and his mother was illiterate. He hadn't even gone to school until he was twelve and that was in a strange country where the language was not his own.

'She always says that a person's value is not measured by what you do in life, or what you know, but by who you are inside. I have noticed that everyone at university seems to be caught up in a powerful conditioning to seek a kind of superficial excitement and hype in life and to almost live for approval and praise from everyone around them. This only leads to constant comparison and competitive behaviour. Do you know anyone who is free from this syndrome?'

None of us could answer 'yes' to this.

'This way of living and being completely ignores the truth of who we are inside ourselves and it just spirals into a neurotic race that can only lead to mental burn out.'

'How do you break the cycle, Mansukh?' I asked him. 'It's so deeply ingrained in us all.'

'More and more I can see just how free my parents are in their simplicity. Mum will sit for hours every day sifting through moong beans one by one and removing all the chaff and stones. I can see her now, sitting on the kitchen floor on some newspaper, going through each grain with her fingers. She is always the absolute image of contentment. I used to sit with her as a child and help her as she sang the ancient songs of her childhood. The haunting melodies captivated my heart and left me spellbound by her presence. To me she seemed like a Goddess, and still does, but I wonder how the world sees her.

'If you were to watch her, even for a moment, performing simple acts *like this you would begin to get a sense of what it must be like to be free of a mind that is agitated and in need of constant gratification and approval.*

'When she makes chappatis she sifts through the flour with her fingers for a long time before she puts the oil into it. It's almost as though she is pouring herself into it, preparing the flour to be receptive. A Westerner might become very irritable waiting for her to 'get on with it'.

Chris was listening intently to Mansukh's words.

'But our culture has conditioned us to believe that what we do is who we are,' he said.

'And that is precisely why people do not value who they are...' Mansukh replied.

Mum

Empower Yourself

———————————— • ————————————

We have lost the value of ourselves and as a result we value things

Do you measure your worth through the eyes of others? If we find ourselves too captured by comparisons with others we can fail to see the power we have as an individual.

Most people's lives are spent within a syndrome of approval and disapproval from others. This means that if someone tells you you're wonderful, you feel great about yourself, and if you are criticised or disapproved of in some way your self esteem takes a dive.

> **Real self esteem is loving who you are from the inside**

Self esteem that's based on approval seeking is very fragile because we are effectively giving our power away to others whenever we feel the need for someone to love or like us. Living is a skill in which you learn to balance how much you give to yourself and how much you give to the outside world.

How can we learn to feel so powerful that we can become independent of needing approval from others? We have to pull in the antennae that are always out there searching for acceptance and give *ourselves* all the approval and love that we need. This will charge us up inside, whereas waiting for others' approval just drains our energy. Real self esteem is loving who you are *from the inside* which completely frees you from the effects of other people's opinions.

We all have a choice as to what will influence us in life. We can choose to live according to others' approval or to *value who we are* - and that is a very powerful thing.

Pathways...

to Empower Your Life

◆ *Make a list of your positive qualities*
It's important to discover what makes you feel happy, worthy and
confident about who you are. This builds a success consciousness.

   * Example: here are twenty reasons for feeling good about myself.

I am a wonderful parent	I love people
I am creative	I am sensitive and caring
I am a loyal friend	I am unique in every way
I work hard at my job	... keep going.

◆ *Consciously be aware of when you are seeking approval*
Ask yourself 'Why?' Then forge a new mental pathway for yourself by
affirming, 'I approve of myself.'

◆ *Value your real nature*
When you act with qualities like compassion and love you attract
them to yourself. These are not just romantic qualities, but powerful
magnetising forces that come from our real nature. We are energetic
beings and all our intentions, motives and thoughts act as 'energy'
magnets for attracting similar energies.
   * Like attracts like, so live as you would like.

◆ *Inversion postures help to change a negative pattern*
Break the approval-seeking pattern by going upside-down every day.
See page 107 for a simple inversion technique.

'But I don't know who I am, Mansukh. That's the problem.' Chris looked sad.

He was in a lot of pain and I could see that Mansukh wanted to help him. 'You need to know that you are much greater than you think you are. You are not your isolated personality, thoughts and feelings but part of something great and vast,' he said.

'It's one thing to say that, but how on earth do you get to experience it when you just don't come up to your own expectations?' Chris looked slightly desperate.

'Mum has found herself by turning inwards, away from the rat race of approval seeking,' Mansukh replied. 'I often watch her as she moves in and out of each moment with such love and almost, you could say, reverence. She gets pleasure and satisfaction from each simple act she performs. Just normal everyday things are completely fulfilling to her.

'Each time we can turn back to ourselves for satisfaction we are chipping away another bit of our old conditioning that is masking who we really are. It's like when Mum puts rice into a big-lipped container and bounces it up into the air. The wind blows away the unwanted chaff and husks leaving only the pure brown rice behind. Or think of the statue makers in Jaipur that my father has told me about. They chip away at bits of marble until all that's left is the divine image of one of the Gods.'

As he was talking I began to realise just how much people need to return to simplicity and to finding joy and laughter in ordinary things. The best times we had ever had together as a group were always when we were sharing the most simple pleasures like playing football or diving into a rugby scrum, silly things that made us feel so wild and free.

'My parents have always taught me to never stop playing and so often I have seen my mother chasing my father up and down the stairs and pinching him all over once she caught him. And Dad is so full of mischief. He is always playing tricks on people; it brings so much fun and laughter to everyone. In forgetting the simple things people have lost touch with who they are.

The Power of Humour

─────────────── • ───────────────

A smile is a curve that sets things straight

Laughter is a part of our nature that is essential to being happy. People may say they have nothing to laugh or smile about, but you can always find something if you look hard enough. Life is full of humour and we just need to retrain ourselves to see with the eyes of a child again.

Look for the humour in every situation

The secret is to develop the 'inner smile'. Develop an attitude that supports and enhances the sunny side of yourself. Become like the little boy who was just putting his shoes on one day when his mother said to him, 'Your shoes are on the wrong feet, Jim!' The little boy looked at this feet, then at his mother in total amazement and said, 'But Mum! These are the only feet I've got!'

We all need to look for the humour in every situation and to learn to laugh at ourselves. The reason we feel so good when we laugh is because we are touching the truest part of ourselves, which is the joy inside us. When we can laugh at life it gives us a much truer perspective that helps us to release our pain and grief about things that are not exactly as we would like them to be. When we can laugh at ourselves and at life we are able to cope with anything that comes our way and we can see the very best in every situation.

Every day we have a choice. We can walk the path of struggle and strife, or the path of joy and laughter.

The secret is to develop the inner smile

Which do you choose?

A Sufi Mystic had remained happy for his whole life. He was always laughing - so much so that he *was* laughter. On his deathbed he was still laughing and his disciples asked him why he was even laughing while dying.

What was funny about death? It had always been confronting to them that he was never sad but now that he was on his deathbed they really felt there was cause for sadness.

"One day I was as sad as you are," he said. " Then I realised it was my choice. Since that day, the first thing I do when I wake up and open my eyes is to say to myself, 'Do you want to be happy or unhappy? What will you choose today?' I always choose happiness."

P a t h w a y s ...

to Cultivating Humour

◆ *Short cuts to a fun-filled day*
  * Reinstate play into your life. Try skipping or playing frisbee.
  * Collect jokes by making a conscious effort to memorise them as you hear them. Make a commitment to tell someone a joke every day.
  * Smile into the mirror at yourself. It will make you laugh!
  * Close your eyes and smile, or make yourself smile for no reason at all.
  * Smile at everyone you meet for no good reason. Try this for a whole hour and watch the difference it makes to your day.
  * Wink at the next person you see. Go on!

◆ *Live joyfully*
  * Think positive, be positive, act positive - it connects you to your innate joy.
  * What activities bring you simple, unaffected joy? Choose at least one of them to do every day.

◆ *Give joy a chance*
  Posture and facial expressions make all the difference.
  Look up, spread your shoulders back, breathe deeply and make a big broad smile. How does it make you feel?
  * Pay attention to your posture and facial expressions during the day.

One of the things that made Mansukh so much fun to be with was his playfulness and he had a wonderful knack of involving other people. I had always associated spirituality with a certain amount of seriousness and had never thought it could be coupled with mischief, but I was wrong. Here was someone who I knew to be very spiritual with a deep understanding of the value of each living moment, someone who had the deepest reverence for life and for people, but who also had such a great respect for the value of playfulness. As I listened to his conversation with Chris, my mind wandered back to our university days and how much we had played together.

There was the time about seven or eight of us had just had supper and on the way out of the refectory started running. I think someone may have said 'Last one up the stairs makes the tea,' or something equally silly. We were chasing each other up three flights of stairs and someone grabbed hold of the first person pulling him over. Soon everyone had fallen down on top of everyone else. Big, hefty lads piled up on top of one another, each trying to get at the other. As soon as someone tried to escape we pulled him back into the centre.

This kind of rugby scrum was a regular event and on wet days could often be seen moving along the upstairs corridor of the hall of residence. On one such day, a particularly 'dirty scrum' had occurred amongst seven or eight huge men. They were all trying to get a hold of Mansukh who had started the whole thing. The noise was absolutely deafening, magnified by the acoustics in the corridor. The great mass started moving up the stairs as hysteria began to set in, but before long we became aware of a kind of 'presence' looming high above us. Peering out of the latticed mass of arms, legs and feet, we were horrified to behold the terrifying vision of the warden, Mrs W. There she stood, feet apart, hands on hips, eyes blazing. Mrs W. was a force to be reckoned with and we disbanded faster than a lorry-load of monkeys.

There was always something wild going on. I remember one day Mansukh was being chased along one of the corridors. As he ran onto the balcony he put his foot on the glass door to stop it and the other guy pushed on the glass. Crash! Then they had to tell the warden. They thought of saying the wind had blown it out but realised no-one in their right mind would believe such a daft story. In the end they went down and casually said, 'You know, there's such a cold draught in the upstairs corridor...'

71

He always stressed how important it was not to laugh at other people's expense however, and never to hurt people with your laughter. 'That is the only time that humour is definitely not beneficial,' he said. 'There is a skill in being able to laugh with people but certainly never at them.'

Today laughter and lightness are the unique hallmark of the Life Foundation, for we always encourage people to celebrate being alive. Our yoga classes and seminars are famous for the laughter and joy they bring into people's lives. Spiritual life for us has never been a serious affair but one that is filled with the spirit of celebration.

Children from a Life yoga class, Sarav, India

Self Esteem

---•---

Discover who you really are

Real self esteem comes from knowing who you are at the essence level. It's a quality of pure charisma that bubbles up from inside us with energy and enthusiasm. It's that irresistible 'something' that is so magnetic and appealing that everybody wants to be around you.

People with low self esteem are identifying with a limited self image based on pure untruth and are unable to value who they are because they choose to hang on to this negative way of seeing themselves.

Laughter reminds us of our inner nature

Our natural charisma is there, buried underneath layers of strange opinions we may have about ourselves. It bursts through in peak moments when we achieve something special like winning the hardest race of our life, or successfully making the most difficult presentation of our career.

Our task is to draw away the veils that mask our inner charisma and the easiest way is to be positive, light-hearted and optimistic, no matter what is happening. Laughter and love are wonderful access routes because they make us remember who we really are.

Self esteem is a quality of pure charisma

Simply put, you have to want to feel positive and happy because it is your true nature. Everything we do in life either supports the truth of who we are or covers it up. Laughter, joyfulness and loving remind us of our inner nature and that is why they feel so good!

73

Pathways...

to Infinite Self Esteem

◆ *Introspection - the easy way to change*
Introspection enables you to **create your own successful responses**
rather than reacting helplessly. Five minutes of introspection can
affect the other 1,435 minutes in your day. What an amazing
exchange rate!

* Last thing at night just before you go to sleep, sit quietly in bed
  and quickly review the events of your day. Please don't judge or
  criticise any of your actions. Just remember them with awareness.

* Now go over some of the things you did really well and try to relive
  them as if you were actually experiencing them again. Really fire
  up your imagination!

* Next, without criticism or judgement, identify events or
  interactions that you would like to improve.

* Replay them in the way you would have liked them to be. For
  example, replace impatience with patience, anger with tolerance,
  or other empowering interactions. Try to relive your new, positive
  response as if you were actually experiencing it.

* Switch off the lights and go to sleep, allowing the subconscious to
  work for you.

If you maintain this daily for three weeks your relationships and self
esteem will improve beyond recognition.

◆ *Reach out to help others*
Generosity always makes you feel better about yourself.
* Send a gift to someone, unannounced, and for no reason at all.
* Go out of your way to make others happy and make them feel
  special.

As the conversation continued, the atmosphere in the room was becoming more and more riveting. I could see Mansukh was beginning to get through and Chris' tension was beginning to melt away.

'Chris, do you remember in our third year I discovered that you could play the guitar?' he said.

'I'll never forget it as long as I live.' Chris looked at me and laughed. 'I had never sung a note in my life and he asked me to sing him a song! I was so shy and nervous and lacking in confidence that I couldn't even open my mouth to try.'

'Do you remember how I closed the curtains and turned my back on you so that you could sing without feeling looked at?' said Mansukh.

'God that was excruciating!' Chris squirmed at the memory. 'I was shaking so much that my fingers got caught up in the guitar strings and the first sound I made was more like a dying gasp than a voice!' Chris has always had a way with words.

'But you did it, didn't you?' he urged.

'Eventually,' he had to admit, 'but only because you pestered me so much.'

Mansukh turned to me. 'I asked Chris to sing over and over again after that until he could do it in front of the others.' Now it made sense. I suddenly remembered one Sunday when we had all been out together. We had piled into a friend's car and ended up on Church Island on the Menai Straits.

We had a bit of a free for all, mucking about and playing frisbee and football until it started to get dark. Then Mansukh asked Chris to get his guitar out of the car. We didn't even know he had one! He asked Chris to sing 'Stairway to Heaven' and we were all simply flabbergasted. It was only now, listening to this conversation that I understood. He had asked him to sing when it was getting dark so that Chris felt safer singing in front of us all. That day must have been a real breakthrough for him.

Today, Chris' singing is legend among those who know him or have come in touch with him through his teaching. His voice and music have brought pleasure and joy to literally thousands of people all over the world.

'You know,' said Mansukh, 'we really can achieve anything if we only choose to believe we can.'

Believe in Yourself

———————————•———————————

You are the most precious gift you will ever possess

Imagine a human being who enters each moment without any hesitation, fear or shyness, but instead settles into the moment, exploring and expanding with it, with kindness and joy. Visualise a human being who is full of happiness and joy, always laughing and smiling, full of enthusiasm and aspiration.

This person is expressing a total belief in himself.

> **Give yourself permission to be what you want to be**

Every human being is endowed with a tremendous power, ability and strength. We have all been given the free will to choose to be happy or sad in each moment, to be confused or clear, full of inspiration or depressed. We always have the choice either to be kind and respectful to others or to despise and challenge them.

We have the ability to choose to believe in *hope* and *faith* as opposed to hopelessness and doubt. We have the choice to look at every challenge in life as a *gift* through which we can transform ourselves and become better, stronger and more peaceful human beings.

This is a simple privilege which does not involve anyone else, for there is no striving for wealth or fame or even dreams for the future. The only thing that is involved is *you, in this moment, now*. You need to give yourself permission to be what you want to be and the first and most important thing is to *stop condemning yourself*.

There is no greater danger for a human being than self-condemnation because it takes away the very essence of power that can make everything happen for you. It takes away inspiration and all possibility of ever succeeding.

76

Two thousand five hundred Gandhian volunteers moved forward and approached the great salt pans which were surrounded by ditches and barbed wire. The volunteers stopped a hundred yards from the stockade and then twenty five unarmed men came forward. The waiting British police shouted a warning for them to stop, but those brave men kept on going. One word of command and scores of police rushed at them, raining blows on their heads with steel-shod clubs.

It takes great strength to follow the path of truth, to walk on when the baton is raised to strike, and not react when it crashes onto your head, your arms, your neck.

The first line of walkers reeled back and were escorted or carried off to have their wounds bandaged. A second line of walkers came. Again the batons flashed in the sun, and again their eyes looked straight on until they fell to the road below. Newsreel films from the day give a vivid portrayal of the faces of the police which changed from initial masks of steel to expressions of discomfort, then pain, and finally - tears. Young men who started the day as hardened soldiers became so broken they were unable to even lift their batons.

The Satyagrahas, as Gandhi's walkers were called, had total and complete faith in themselves. With such faith a small group of unarmed walkers shook the might of the British Government to its roots.

This is the power of Believing in Yourself.

Pathways...

to Total Faith in Yourself

◆ ***Build a foundation of small steps to success***
Think of a goal you would like to achieve in life.
* What is the ***smallest and easiest*** action that will help you to get there?
* Commit yourself to taking an action like this every day.
You will soon build an energy of success that will empower you to take larger and larger strides towards your goals.

◆ ***Hopping Meditation***
* Imagine you are inside a circle.

* Think about everything that you are now, and especially everything that holds you back in life.

* Now visualise another circle next to you that contains all the qualities that you would like to have. See it glowing with light and the energy of success.

* Now take a leap into the second circle leaving all your limitations behind.

Congratulations! You have just helped to reprogramme your body's neuromuscular memory and tricked your mind out of an old groove. Repeat this meditation every day or whenever you feel a little despondent about yourself.

Mansukh carried on. 'It all depends on the way you think. Mum always said that people simply do not realise how powerful their thoughts are. If they did they would be very careful which ones they allowed into their mind.

'A Russian scientist called Fyadov once carried out extensive tests to determine the power of thought. In one experiment he arranged to 'send' a thought from Moscow where he was, to Tiflis, a thousand miles away.

'At an appointed time he concentrated his mind and projected the thought 'go to sleep' to his friend. Sure enough, the man fell into a deep sleep. Then he thought, 'wake up within five minutes' and he did, only slightly stunned and confused.'

'But most of our thoughts are on automatic aren't they?' I asked.

'They do spring up automatically from the hosts of subconscious beliefs and attitudes we have acquired during our life, but we also have a choice. When you start consciously choosing what thoughts you have, then you are taking charge of your mind and therefore your life.

'Think kindly. Think great. And that's what you will become, because the way you think determines the way you feel. You can decide to change your mind.'

'Is it really so simple, Mansukh? Is changing my mind really powerful enough to get me out of this space?' Chris looked doubtful.

'The universe is totally positive, which means it can only ever respond to us positively. In simple terms this means that whatever you are thinking, the universe has to say 'Yes!''

That special evening spent exploring one man's life, his fears, hopes and aspirations, is one I shall never forget. That night I witnessed a miracle as Chris transformed before my very eyes. Is this the power of an indigenous person's life and insight? Once again I felt grateful to Mansukh and his parents for their deep concern to make changes....

Your Thoughts Create your World

•

You are the creator of your own destiny

Just as within the heart of a tiny atom lies the power to create and also the power to destroy, every single thought we have contains the same potential of creation - or destruction. As thousands of thoughts rise up in our minds every day it's easy to be unaware of their power, but each and every thought is a potent instrument for shaping the experience of our daily lives.

> **The universal echo is YES! YES! YES!**

The most powerful tool we have at our disposal is our thinking mind - *when we take charge of it.* Using the power of the mind to work *for us* we can disempower our negative tendencies and empower the highest attitudes and beliefs so that everything becomes possible for us and nothing is beyond our reach.

There is only one echo reverberating through the universe and that is YES! YES! YES! This echo is constantly responding to the commands we put out. Whatever thoughts we have, the universal response will always be a positive one. This means that if you are thinking that your life is a struggle you will have 100% back-up from the universe, because it agrees with whatever you say.

Positive thinking is so powerful because we are effectively aligning ourselves with all the forces of creation and are empowered accordingly. Likewise, of course, the negative thoughts and attitudes we project out from ourselves will be equally empowered.

It's not easy if we've been conditioned to think negatively all our lives but it is good to remember that as soon as we start changing the way we think, the universe is right there behind us saying 'Yes!'

80

P a t h w a y s ...

to the Power of Thought

◆ ***Take a simple thought like 'I can'***
It has been medically shown that this thought sets off enzyme reactions that change and prepare the body and emotions for positive results. Similarly 'I cannot' actually weakens the body's vitality and strength.

◆ ***'Yes I can!'***
Try saying 'Yes I can!' every day. There is no power greater than self enthusiasm.

◆ ***Try it for yourself***
Ask a friend to muscle test you while you think 'I can'.

◆ ***Muscle Testing***
* Hold your arm up sideways and, while your friend presses down lightly on the top of your outstretched hand, gently resist the pressure. This allows your friend to determine your natural strength.

* Now let them repeat the test while you mentally repeat 'I cannot' at least ten times to yourself. The results are self evident.

* Test again, this time thinking 'I can' so deeply and powerfully that every cell in your body comes alive with the feeling of 'I can'. How strong is your arm now?

Witness the power of your thoughts!

P a t h w a y s ...

to Powerful Thoughts

Monkeys in India are always hopping and jumping
around, harassing everyone in sight, but as soon as they have hold of
a banana or orange they immediately calm down and stop annoying
people. Our mind, like the monkey, needs something to keep it in
check. Repetition of positive words and affirmations creates a
powerful anchor that can focus the mind and help us to gain
mastery over our thoughts and feelings. Written affirmations
penetrate even more deeply into the subconscious, especially if done
at night just before sleeping.

◆ *Affirmations*
Affirm means 'to make firm'. Use the power of your thoughts to
work for you by using words that erase negative thoughts and
counteract the old negative conditioning.

◆ *Suggested affirmations:*

Life is on my side	I am full of charisma
I am wonderful	I am totally successful now
I can achieve anything	I love and approve of myself exactly as I am

◆ *Hint*
Do not worry if you find your affirmation hard to believe at first. Just
say it out loud, sing it or write it down. For maximum effect do all
three!
Remember that whatever you say or think you will attract to yourself,
so think high and think big.

Pathways...

to Words of Power

◆ Since time immemorial, sacred words have been used in every tradition to change one's mental state. 'Mantra' means 'The word that frees and protects.'

Here are a few mantras you could choose from:

Buddhist	Om Mane Padme Hum	*Invokes your infinite potential*
	Na Mu Myo Ho Ren Ge Kyo	*May all attain Peace*
Christian	Alleluia	*Praise the Lord*
	Kyrie Eleison	*Brings compassion & mercy*
Hindu	Sri Ram (Gandhi's mantra)	*Creates truth and compassion*
	Om Namoh Shivaya	*Invokes the highest will & calms anger*
Islam	Allah, Allah	*God, God*
Jewish	Shalom, Shalom	*Peace, Peace*
Native American	Hey Yanga, Ho Yanga, Hey Yung Yung	*Honour the Earth Mother*

◆ Use these mantras in exactly the same way as you would use any affirmation, repeating them as often as you can, wherever you can, and particularly in moments of quiet or meditation.

Gandhi once said, 'Mantra becomes one's staff of life and carries one through every ordeal. Each repetition has a new meaning, each repetition carries you closer to God.'

That night I lay in bed, my mind full of thoughts, feelings and inspirations. My yearning to really experience what Mansukh was talking about seemed to be growing deeper and stronger every day. The more he talked about the 'greatness' of a human being the more I wanted to know it. I could feel the truth in his words but still the gates of my own feelings of limitation seemed permanently closed around me.

'There has to be a way to really break through those barriers of self limitation, a way to taste the power and strength that Gandhi and King had tapped into.' My voice sounded strangely intense.

Mansukh was always so relaxed about things. It must have been all the yoga he did, but he just smiled and said, 'Yes.'

'Is it a secret?' I was determined to get to it somehow.

'Of course not, John,' he said. 'For the last few years we have all been slowly getting used to the idea that we are each something much more than we thought we were. The experiences we have shared together as a group have demonstrated the intense power that is generated by even pointing yourself in that direction. But, as Dad has stressed over and over again to me throughout my life, spirituality has to be action oriented. It's not about sitting around dreaming of your greatness. It's getting out there into the community and demonstrating spirituality at grass roots level, meeting people, sharing with others, helping those in need. The one thing the greatest people in history have in common is their passion for serving others. Gandhi's greatness lay in his love for the people of India. He wanted to help them over and above anything else in his life.'

Mansukh looked at me very directly.

'If you really want to make your spirituality come alive in your life then get out there and help people in any way you can.'

Finding Your Greatness

———————————————————— • ————————————————————

What is it that makes people great?

People like Gandhi and Martin Luther King stand out because they realised they were unlimited in their ability to achieve their goals. No matter what obstacles came in front of them, they never allowed feelings of inadequacy, limitation or despondency to deter them. As a result of this they were both able to create vast, sweeping changes in the world and their efforts have created ripples that still continue to inspire us all.

The truth is we are all great

We will always be successful in the area in which we have realised the truth of our greatness most fully. A millionaire will have a total belief in his ability to acquire wealth. A surgeon feels confident he can pay minute attention to detail or to keep his hand steady and mind clear at the edge of life and death. So what is the difference between the millionaire, the surgeon, the Gandhis of this world and us?

Only the limitation games we choose to play and the choices we make. The truth is we are all great and we need to continually affirm our greatness and uphold the hero and heroine within us.

We will always be successful in the area in which we have realised the truth of our greatness most fully

85

P a t h w a y s ...

to Finding Your Greatness

◆ *Discovering your greatness*
Don't look for big signs of your greatness, it's right there in the little ones! When you create success in small interactions you touch your greatness.
* Make a list of everything that you know you can do well, no matter how large or small. Each one is an area where you are touching your greatness. Congratulate yourself!

◆ *Greatness lies within*
In your quietest times listen deeply to what your heart tells you. When you have a great idea follow it up immediately. Remember, your greatness is only a choice away.

◆ *Regularly count your blessings*
Appreciation has a magnetic power of attraction.
* Every morning say, 'Three things I really appreciate in my life are...'
* Create encounters with beauty. Watch the sunset from your balcony, spend five minutes watching children playing... the possibilities are endless.

◆ *Think, walk and talk as if you are great...*
* Who inspires you most?
* Observe how they walk, how they talk, the words and gestures they use and the thoughts they express. If you don't know them personally, research them in books or on film.
* Spend one hour imitating as many of the characteristics of this person as you can. How do you feel at the end of the hour? Now try another hour!

Gandhi was waiting. The atmosphere throughout India was becoming increasingly violent as the British Government's laws seemed to be crushing the life out of the Indian people. The salt tax was the final blow. Gandhi knew that working class unrest could easily result in violence at any moment and everyone was urging him to do something.

Still he waited to hear what he called 'the inner voice'. He sat and listened for six weeks while the whole of India hovered on the verge of an armed rebellion and no amount of pressure could persuade him to make a hasty decision.

On March 12th he got up from his prayers and started walking towards Dandi. Together with eighty seven men and women from his ashram he walked from village to village. Several times a day they stopped to hold meetings and prayers as he urged people to wait for his signal. In every village more people joined the march so that by the time he reached Dandi he had accumulated a non-violent army of several thousand strong.

What was he going to do? The atmosphere was electric as thousands of people stayed up all night to pray on the beach and as the sun began to rise Gandhi stood up. He walked down to the sea, dipped himself in, and then returned to the beach. Kneeling down he gently picked up some salt left by the waves on the water's edge and held it up in his hand.

A small, frail old man, outlined against the warm colours of the rising sun, his hand held high in the air, representing India's symbol for freedom. A simple act that brought the sun down on the British Empire.

'That's it! I've got it!' I was so excited that I had burst into Mansukh's room in the middle of the night. My enthusiasm must have been infectious because before long everyone had crowded into the room to find out what the excitement was all about. 'It's our first ever project,' I explained. 'We're going to collect food and money so that we can give the old people a Christmas hamper each.'

I had been surveying an old couple's house that day for the council and when I left them I'd asked them what they wanted for Christmas. 'A Christmas pudding would be nice,' the old lady had smiled at me wistfully and I suddenly realised that they probably didn't even have enough money to buy one. I'd been thinking all evening about what to do for them.

'There must be hundreds of old couples like them,' I said, 'and we could make this year really special by giving them a box of food, couldn't we?' It felt like a really brilliant idea and everyone immediately went for it. Since the students were all going home for Christmas, and many of them were self catering, we reckoned they might have some spare tins of food to donate. The response was quite astounding. Not only did they give their spare food but many of them actually went out and bought food especially for us. Although we didn't ask for cash, people kept giving us money.

By the end of the weekend we had a small mountain of food and with the money we raised we went to the local cash and carry and bought Christmas puddings. We'd also collected loads of cardboard boxes to pack the food into. We spent all the next week packing shoe boxes until we couldn't move in the sitting room because it was so full.

As a child I had once been involved with delivering harvest festival hampers to old people. The amazing feeling that it gave me has never left me so I wanted to give some underprivileged children the same opportunity to experience the power of giving.

We knew the girl who ran the local Community Action children's club in one of the poorer areas of town. She brought about a dozen youngsters in a minibus to help us load up the hampers and spend the day delivering to all the old people on our list. As we went round each house it was a wonderful feeling to see the old people's faces. They just weren't expecting to be given anything. It meant a lot to them, and to us.

*My Relationship
with Others*

By now it was becoming very clear that we needed a bigger place where we could all be together and be more able to focus ourselves and our energy.

Everyone had a bit of money to chip in and between us we raised about £1,500 for a deposit. John went with a friend to look at an old miner's cottage in Gerlan. It wasn't at all suitable, but walking back up the hill, an old Welsh man popped his head out from his doorway and said, 'Are you looking for a house to buy?'

For some reason he had assumed they were. 'I know a house just over there,' he said, pointing at a row of terraced houses. 'I've got the keys if you are interested.' It belonged to a friend of his.

He took them in straight away and although it was small it was well done up and very homely. He told them that his friend wanted £7,000 which seemed just about the right price. We called it Pinewood. It was just an old slate miner's cottage and none of us could have anticipated at that time exactly what was going to grow from such a humble beginning.

We discovered such a power in living together for personal and spiritual growth and began to learn how to really appreciate the positivity and the best within ourselves so that we could bring the best out in others. For me personally, Pinewood catalysed the power and dignity of human trust. We found that by living together in total trust we became very secure within ourselves. When you lose insecurity you lose fear which means that we were able to act very naturally with each other and just be ourselves. This brought us a great feeling of joy and fun in being together.

We instinctively knew what Mother Teresa upholds so strongly - that a family that prays together stays together - and it was around this time that we started a regular prayer ceremony every morning and night called the Aarati.

The Aarati is an ancient ceremony from my parents' tradition. It involves a small butter lamp with five flames. Each flame represents one of the five senses, the means by which we experience the world. The Aarati purifies the senses so that we can perceive more clearly the divinity that is in the world. I suppose it could be compared to washing your windows on a spiritual level. It became a very powerful tool for us to defuse conflicts and disagreements and brought us together every day in such a way that we were regularly sharing what was common to us all. It also provided an opportunity to sing together, play instruments and share the most joyful aspects of worship.

It seemed as though the gentleness in us all, combined with an inner drive to discover something so amazing it would shake us to our roots, gave our home its purpose and function.

We realised the time had come to share what was precious to us within the community and began teaching yoga and meditation on a regular basis. It felt very special to begin to share what we had found to be such a powerful force for health and healing in our lives. We began to see more clearly that our purpose lay in sharing ourselves with others and that we had not just come together for our own spiritual growth and well-being.

Mansukh

When Rita arrived at Bangor station nobody knew she was coming. She had written to say she was going to spend a weekend with us but had forgotten to mention which weekend. Not to be deterred by the lack of reception, Rita made her way to seek out Mansukh at the university where she found him in his research department.

He was more than a little surprised to see her but very pleasantly so, and took her back to Pinewood. They decided to go for a walk together to discuss the problems she was having in her life and as they were walking up an old track a very large woman on horseback suddenly shouted angrily at them, 'You are not allowed to park up here!'

Rita was furious and immediately retaliated, 'How dare you talk to us like that?'

Before the woman could reply, Mansukh gently intervened. 'We are so sorry,' he said, 'we really didn't know.'

Rita told me later that he said it with so much sincerity that the woman was completely disarmed. All she could do was to turn her horse around and trot away! Rita couldn't quite believe it and asked Mansukh how he could be so nice to such an aggressive person.

'I don't think she understood the situation,' he said quietly. I think Rita was very impressed with this incident, coming as she did from a rough area of London where she worked in an Advice Centre for the Asian communities. She was quite a crusader for Asian women and used to holding her own in any difficult situation.

Today, Rita relates to people with the same kind of skill and unconditional love that she witnessed on that day.

It wasn't long before Rita joined us, adding her unique strength and enthusiasm as well as her natural flair for leadership to the group. She loved the intensity of our way of life and the idea of a spiritual community really seemed to appeal to her. She'd been meditating for many years on her own by now and had recognised how much easier it is to grow and evolve spiritually with other people who have the same aspiration. She travelled up every weekend from London to join in our meetings either in Pinewood or Mum and Dad's in Fraser Street.

The next addition to our growing community was Lobsang, the cat. Chris brought her home one day from his parents and convinced us that we simply must have her. She was a cross between a tortoiseshell and every other kind of cat you could imagine, with black and ginger over one eye and white spotted stripy bits over the other. Mansukh decided right from the start that Lobsang was not going to set a bad example by lolling around all day. He had a habit of sneaking up on her as she lay sleeping peacefully on the sofa and slowly insinuating his hand underneath her belly. The next thing she knew she was waking up in mid air! He did this just about every time he saw her until she became so alert that as soon as anyone walked in the room her eyes would open instantly and she always positioned herself so that she could see exactly what was going on! She did love him, and to prove it she climbed onto his lap one day and gave birth to four little kittens!

Lobsang wasn't the only one who was kept on the alert. Only six months after we had settled in, our old friend Jas from university came to visit us. We were discussing how we really needed a bigger place where more people could come and take part in what we were doing and during the conversation Jas said, 'It's all very well talking about it, but what are you going to do about it?'

That was it. The very next day found us all out on the road - literally! We put our thumbs out and started hitching. Our aim was to let the universe guide us to wherever we needed to be. By now we had a clearer idea that we wanted somewhere we could start teaching yoga and meditation. We had no idea where we were going or what exactly we were looking for; we simply trusted that we were going to find it.

That night Chris found himself in the Northampton YMCA where he discovered that the warden was an old friend he hadn't seen since they were at school together. Chris ended up in Birmingham working as a teacher, whilst living with Mum and Dad in Bilston. He still swears that his choice had nothing to do with Mum's cooking.

I found myself working in Oxford with another friend while we looked around for properties but we eventually ended up looking in the Midlands because it was central to most places and property was relatively cheap.

One day when Chris and I were driving up Dover Street in Bilston I saw a huge house on the corner and said to Chris, 'That would be ideal for us.' It wasn't for sale as far as we could see but, as it turned out, Dad knew the owner, a Mr Ram.

Mr Ram wanted to move to India, as luck would have it, and being a friend of Dad's, decided to sell us his house at a ridiculously low price. He wanted £16,600 and between us we had managed to raise £7,500 in cash.

As the house was not mortgageable Mr Ram offered us a very unusual deal. He accepted an initial down payment of £7,500 and a promise to pay the further £9,100 over a period of twelve months at £175 a week. This was a great deal of money to us in those days and it meant pooling virtually all our combined wages leaving very little to spare for living on. For some reason we agreed to this very unorthodox transaction which was really only based on mutual trust. We moved in straight away and then our work began in earnest.

Maristowe had to be completely gutted and rebuilt. I moved down and got a job in the County Court while Chris was still teaching in Birmingham. Everyone else had jobs in different locations to raise the money to pay off the loan and only one person was able to work full time on the house.

After working all day everyone came home and put on their overalls and started working on the house straight away. At that time everything was just a mass of dust and rubble so that my posh County Court suit had to be carefully wrapped in polythene and hung in the wardrobe which stood all alone upstairs amidst the gathering debris.

Mansukh came down every weekend to help as he was still studying in Bangor and it was around this time that Rita moved into Maristowe. She soon became 'one of the lads', shovelling rubble with her unique kind of strength and zestful enthusiasm. We were all sleeping in one room upstairs and when we were changing the windows the snow came in and covered our sleeping bags with a white icy blanket in the night.

We had hardly any money as every penny had to go towards paying off our debt to Mr Ram, so we lived on porridge and baked beans for over a year. What could have made Rita want to walk into this? The truth is that there was such an atmosphere at that time that is almost impossible to describe. We were all feeling that we were part of something that was immeasurably exciting and, despite the hardships, everyone approached the project with a spirit of joy and almost relish. We didn't have time for depressions or disputes and we could all sense that we were not just building a house but a future for many people we had not yet met. It gave us zest and energy that appeared to be endless. Many times I was so tired I fell asleep on the bus coming home. Often I fell off the seat when the bus went around a corner, but as soon as I got home my tiredness would disappear and I could work half the night again. It was like that. Something unseen and immense was driving us all.

*Maristowe
in the early days
Bilston, 1981*

Left to right:
Chris, Rita, John, Ian

Maristowe House

John and little Pravin

In the beginning

Relating to Other People

———————————— • ————————————

'Love is a rare herb that makes a friend out of a sworn enemy.'
M.K. Gandhi

Our whole life revolves around relationships. The people we are nearest to, children, friends, colleagues at work or people we meet on the street, all show us exactly where we are at with ourselves by the quality of our interaction with them.

Possibly the greatest mistake people make is to blame others for the way they are feeling. It is true that some personalities can be very testing and others very pleasing to relate to but, at the end of the day, each one of us is responsible for the way we react to each other.

You get back what you put into life

When we can see the world and everyone in it as a mirror, relating to other people takes on a whole new meaning. We all have experienced those days when we feel so good, the birds are singing, the sky is blue and everyone we meet seems to be smiling. Why is that? It's because *we* are smiling. If you smile into a mirror, your image smiles back, and it's the same if you frown.

Life creates a beautiful background for us to see ourselves and know where our maximum growth lies. When we can understand that the universe is constantly moving us closer towards our true self we can choose to see each event in our life in a positive way, for every situation and encounter helps us to grow a little more towards that awareness.

In our heart of hearts we all want to get on well with everyone but the reality is often a challenge! We all know when we are getting it right because our relationships are stimulating, creative and expanding. We also know when we are missing it because we experience strain, tension, frustration and pain in our interactions.

98

What an incredible time in our lives. Building Maristowe was a real dream for us and proved to be a crucial landmark in our history. It was almost like building our first big spiritual battery. Life had become a whirl of constant activity as we got up early to go to work, came home, worked all evening and often through the night.

The whole place was like a building site for months on end and we had hardly anything to eat and only a little stove to cook on. Sleep was an even rarer commodity than food because we were always working to deadlines. We targeted a date by which we had to finish a particular job and this often meant staying up all night for several nights in a row.

Many times I staggered into the County Court having had no sleep at all and somehow managed to get through the day without falling asleep at my desk. The constant, nonstop activity was very hard work but we were all happy even though on one level life was completely crazy.

The opportunity was there to really give everything we had to whatever we were doing. We knew we were building a future for thousands of people and it gave us so much energy and enthusiasm. It wasn't physical energy that kept us going; it was the energy you get from giving all of yourself to something you believe in. It wasn't just hard work; it was work dedicated to the very highest purpose and done with that in mind.

I enjoyed everything I was doing and after a while just lost touch with my physical state, as though drunk on some divine substance. I felt fulfilled and full in the sense that there was no part of me lacking or wanting for anything. At last I had found what Mansukh had told me about all those years ago - that special feeling of utter and complete contentment.

It was quite illogical but here amidst the dust and rubble, working in freezing conditions with very little sleep, I had found it. What more proof did I need that happiness was an internal experience and not related to any external circumstances?

Unknowingly, I had prayed for this on the mountain as I held onto my father. Something inside had cried out to understand what life is really about. I had yearned to touch the highest within me so that I could rise with the wind of fate, instead of being destroyed by it. I had needed to understand, and to help others to really comprehend, that life is trying to lead us and not mislead us. I had to discover what we are really capable of experiencing within ourselves and to know that a much greater reality does lie inside us, just waiting to be tapped into.

I was discovering that service, or 'karma yoga' as the yogis call it, is an incredible highway to that inner space. Working for the good of the whole and not just for oneself opens us up to the very highest part of ourselves straight away. Maristowe taught me that it isn't something you have to build up to over many years. It happens the moment you engage in selfless action and give up self seeking.

The very first room we worked on was the meditation room because we knew it was to become the heart of our spiritual community. We recognised instinctively that once that heart began to beat everything else would fall into place.

We had to knock down a dividing wall in order to make this room, but we had agreed with Mr Ram that we wouldn't make any structural changes until we had paid off our last instalment on the house. This event became a great source of anticipation for us as the months went by. We finished all the other jobs that had to be done like fitting the windows, plastering the walls and laying the floor and finally the great day arrived. I had just paid the final instalment, I remember, and couldn't wait to get back to give the signal to 'go for it'. There was such an excitement in everyone as we armed ourselves with mallets and hammers to start knocking the wall down.

This experience turned out to be very special for me, not just because we had all been looking forward to it, but because of what happened to me personally in the process. It was one of those experiences that were so magical they can never be forgotten. We started to knock down the wall and with each blow of the hammer I became increasingly aware of something within me working through me. I was watching the body move and act and I was aware of the mind thinking but it was as if I was behind it all. It was like being in a state of bliss and as I watched the bricks fall I was seeing it from inside this body, yet not identifying with it at all. I experienced a kind of joy that bubbles up inside you and makes you want to laugh, although it's not excitable laughter. It's something else.

I know now that I was experiencing what the Gita describes as the shift of consciousness from our everyday identification with our body and mind to identification with the indwelling Self, the Real Self.

Empowering Relationships

---•---

Look for the best and you'll find it

Who brings out the very best in you? Isn't it always those people who accept, value and respect you for who you are?

When we can support others to feel good about themselves it releases them from the need to put others down. People only diminish others when they themselves are uncertain about their own worth. Those with high self esteem who are secure about their own value always empower others and *never put them down.*

> **Empower the highest in others and it empowers you**

If you look at any great leader or pioneer you will see this quality of respect for others. People like Martin Luther King, Mahatma Gandhi and Mother Teresa all share a genius for making people feel good about themselves - even the lowliest of people.

Their attitude of seeing the very highest in everyone has won them the love and loyalty of millions of people. There is no need to manipulate others to get them to perform well; you simply need to put strength and energy into empowering them.

> **Choose to see the best in people**

The moment we try to manipulate people we are lost. Living a life without manipulation creates quite a different environment from the one in which we are always planning and scheming.

101

I think that Dad was really proud of us as a group of young people who were aspiring to live up to a set of ideals. During our first few years at Maristowe House, which was only a few minutes walk from his own home, he very much took us under his wing. Hardly a day would pass without him coming around morning and evening, making himself available to answer questions about our practice or even sort out potential problems. His depth of knowledge never ceased to amaze me. But Dad also had a mischievous sense of humour which kept us all on our toes.

For some time he had been telling us about what I can only describe as a kind of yogic underwear that was especially helpful when practising yoga asanas. He explained how beneficial it was and suggested that we try it out.

Game for anything, I asked Dad if he could make one for me. A few days later he produced from his bag the much awaited garment. It consisted of a 'T' shaped piece of simple cotton fabric which was used to gird the loins. The next day I tried it out in the morning yoga practice and found it really very comfortable, so much so, in fact, that I decided to keep it on for the rest of the day whilst I went to work. What I hadn't realised was that Dad had made the 'tail' of the garment much longer than was necessary which meant that it was quite tricky to tuck in neatly.

At the time I was working as a Clerk of Court in the local County Court. The court offices had at least thirty staff who attended to various administrative duties. That day I had a lot of filing to do and so I was standing at a bank of cabinets in the centre of the office. I had just returned from the toilet when I suddenly became aware that the normal buzz of office activity had given way to an unusual hush. I had an uncomfortable sense that I had become the centre of my colleagues' attention. Having visited the toilet I had failed to tuck the yard or so of superfluous fabric into my trousers and it now hung down behind me like a white tail. Just then my office manager, who had joined me by the filing cabinets, gave my exposed underwear two sharp tugs. 'Joined the Bunny Club have we, John?' he asked.

To say that I was embarrassed would be an understatement. It took me a few days to recover sufficiently to even tell anyone about it. Dad roared with laughter when I told him and slapped me on the back as he usually did on such occasions. Then almost immediately his face changed as he looked me in the eyes and said, 'You know, John, they don't realise how lucky they are to have someone like you working with them.' There was such a feeling of sincere love in his words that I couldn't help but feel uplifted and special. He wasn't going to allow the incident to diminish me in any way and was making a point of building me up. He had that ability to make you feel good about yourself through the love and acceptance he extended.

Once again, I feel grateful that he was a part of my life.

John filming in Australia during the Friendship Without Frontiers world tour

P a t h w a y s ...

Have the Right Attitude

◆ *Look for the best*

So begin by always looking for the very best qualities in people. It's so easy to see what is 'wrong' with people but this kind of attitude creates a contraction within us and them and makes communication very difficult. When you choose to see the best in everyone, especially those who are confronting you in your life, it draws the best out of you!

◆ *Power struggles*

Be brave enough to tell people they are strong and not weak because people's problems arise out of feeling weak. It makes them seek power and strength in order to feel secure. When you feel weak you want power over people but if you are already strong your power comes from within instead.

If you are not seeking power over others you will feel no need to impose upon anyone and instead you can simply appreciate and love them. Give people the chance to be themselves, no matter who they are. Be accepting and forgiving and you will feel comfortable with people. Once you begin to accept yourself, then you can move on to accept others as they are - unconditionally. Don't take away from people. Give to them, for what you give comes back to you ten thousandfold.

There were many special people with us while we were building Maristowe who stayed for a while and then moved on to other things. Each one of them made a unique and unforgettable contribution to our lives.

One very dear friend of mine was called Ian. He was a real character and I always felt very close to him right from the start and he left a deep and lasting impression on us all. Ian was a master craftsman, especially with wood and, in fact, most of the woodwork in Maristowe is infused with his loving care. He was a great friend to everyone and taught us all many different things. One of his greatest qualities was his complete and utter fearlessness, and he had a unique way of working with other people's fear.

Often when people came to help with the building work he tried to give them the confidence to do things they never dreamed they were capable of. He used to say that the only way to overcome fear was to face it, and I'll never forget the day he coaxed Rita onto the roof.

Rita had never even been up a ladder in her life before and suddenly here she was three stories up forty feet above the ground.

I could hear Ian empowering her to do it. 'Now listen,' he was saying, 'if this ladder was on the ground you wouldn't think twice about stepping from one rung to another. Just because you are forty feet up in the air it shouldn't make any difference. You are quite capable of doing it.' His words were gently reassuring her as she got to the top of the ladder and saw she was going to have to swing her leg off the ladder to get on to the roof. Ian said casually, 'Just swing your leg up!'

'No!' said Rita

'Just do it, it'll be fine,' he said. Next thing you knew she was crawling up the roof on all fours to help him fix a ridge tile in place while he just walked casually up. But she did it! I don't think Rita will ever forget the day she faced, and overcame, fear.

Ian taught me a lot personally about fearlessness simply because he didn't appear to have much fear of anything. In his youth he had done many things like hanging upside-down under bridges, scaling the Eiffel tower and other death defying feats. What I learned from him was very important because so often in life we don't do things because of the fear of failure. More often than not that fear is completely unfounded and when we face it head on we find that we can do it.

The Transformation of Fear

---•---

'Fearlessness is the first requisite of spirituality.'
M.K. Gandhi

Fear binds and suffocates our ability to build strong and fulfilling relationships with people. The fears can be endless - fear of losing someone, fear of feelings they may bring up in us, fear that they may see us for who we are (or think we are).

> **It is necessary to have an unshakeable faith in oneself**

It is necessary to have an unshakeable faith in oneself as a powerful person and a conviction that our inner security is strong and independent of other people's actions.

It is only when we resolve to see the very best in people that we will be able to trust them instead of fearing them. We will learn to trust that they are not out to get us, but that they are the same as we are. Everyone is seeking the same things in life. Everyone wants to be able to communicate without fear and to be loved and respected for who they are.

Another antidote to fear is to recognise that people only do what they do because they are trying to feel better and to ease their own pain. Knowing this helps us to understand people's behaviour, no matter how strange.

When we can understand where people are coming from we will find that we will lose our own fear. It's all about developing the right attitude to the way we relate to people. It's a question of breaking down the barriers of fear, letting go of anger or hatred and allowing the natural love inside us to come through.

106

Pathways...

to the End of Fear

Facing fear
There is no short-cut to overcoming fear. Whatever you are afraid of, you must face it. Never run away from your fears.

How you feel about yourself makes all the difference
Build up your body so that it feels strong and confident. Choose not to see the world through a window of fear but look through the eyes of love, trust and faith in yourself.

Fear only exists in the past or the future
Sustained attention to the breath brings you into the moment. Follow your breath in and out.

Relaxation
Relaxation programmes help you to let go of fear and stressful thoughts.

Break the patterns of fear
Invert your body. Lie down and put your legs up against the wall. Breathe in and hold for a few seconds until you feel the pattern change. (If you have a heart condition do not hold your breath.)

Acknowledge your fear
* Ask yourself the question, 'What am I afraid of?'
* Work out a simple way to overcome it.
* Look for the support of a friend if you need it.

Do not add to your fear by imagining it
Focus on being courageous.

Satyagraha week was the highlight of our lives. From time to time the whole group would stop whatever they were doing to take time off to spend a week at Pinewood together in retreat.

For a whole seven days we immersed ourselves in the teachings of Mahatma Gandhi which centred around the power of non-violence and fearlessness. Dad was always in jubilant spirits during these times because he loved nothing better than to talk about the great Mahatma. When he spoke about him it was always in his own language and Mansukh translated for us.

'He was a rare individual,' he told us. 'He epitomised the great power and strength of a human being, yet at the same time he had such a quality of loving kindness that was almost like soft down around his iron will. In that respect, he had it all, both the strength of will to achieve his goals and the love and kindness to melt the hearts of millions.'

Dad brought Gandhi alive for us, so much so that we could almost feel the presence of that great man in the room with us.

'Gandhi taught me,' he continued, his small body alive and vibrant as he spoke, 'to really believe that inside us there is an incredible power that allows us to meet any situation. You must see and realise that power so that you can achieve your ideals in just the same way that he did.'

He stressed the importance of following the laws of the universe by really living the values of ahimsa or non-violence and truth.

'Gandhi has proved by his example,' he told us, 'that when you follow the natural laws, you are crowned by the grace of God.'

He looked at us all, his eyes full of dynamic stillness, and said, 'This man has written the history of peace. Follow his example, live like he did. Keep God alive in your lives through simple, prayerful living and you will never go wrong.'

Gandhi was a great inspiration to us all and because Dad had known and worked with him his influence had always been very strong in his life. He had never known anything else but to live by the ideals of a Satyagraha.

'Satya' means truth and comes from 'Sat' which means quite simply, 'that which is'. He told us, 'Truth alone exists. For truth is not what holds good just at a certain time, but that which never changes. All other negative expressions like greed, hatred, evil and injustice are only born if we all give them the space to be. If we don't support them, they cannot exist. There is not one negative emotion that can ever exist without our

participation and permission.'

This was such a powerful teaching for me, because I could sense the freedom that could come from definitely refusing to associate with negativity. Gandhi's life epitomised his association with truth and this was where his great power lay.

We adopted Gandhi's holistic model for an ideal society, portrayed by the qualities written inside his Satyagraha Lotus. Its petals represent the tools he used to implement his model in India, and we created our own to fit our western society.

That man I love who is incapable
Of ill will, and returns love for hatred.
Living beyond the reach of *I* and *mine*,
And of pain and pleasure, full of mercy,
Contented, self-controlled, of firm resolve,
With all his heart and all his mind given
To Me - with such a one I am in love.

Not agitating the world, nor by it
Agitated, he stands above the sway
Of elation, competition and fear,
Accepting life, good and bad, as it comes.
He is pure, efficient, detached, ready
To meet every demand I make on him
As a humble instrument of My work. . . .

Who serves both friend and foe with equal love,
Not buoyed up by praise, nor cast down by blame,
Alike in heat and cold, pleasure and pain,
Free from selfish attachments and self-will,
Ever full, in harmony everywhere,
Firm in faith - such a one is dear to Me.

Bhagavad Gita, Chp. 12

Trials and tribulations became the stepping stones for our spiritual growth and we soon realised they were there to make us stronger not weaker and were just as necessary as the easy times.

We set ourselves targets for accomplishing each task which created situations where each one of us came up against our own personal limits over and over again. We had to constantly break through the limits of how much we felt we could endure, especially around the issue of lack of sleep, because in order to meet our deadlines we sometimes found ourselves up all night for many nights in a row. This meant we had to draw on completely new resources of energy we didn't even know that we had.

Every phase we went through taught us that it wasn't what we were physically that really mattered, but how we felt inside. The inner world was taking over to such a degree that we began to lose track of everything else. Although our bodies were moving, acting and working constantly, that wasn't the biggest focus.

We all had our personal and group challenges but each time we resolved them with the help of the teachings of people like Gandhi, Krishna or Saint Francis. The more we drew on their ideas the more vibrant was our strength and creativity and the more an uncanny divine force came into play.

There is one teaching in the Bhagavad Gita that became our guiding light at this time. 'Do your allotted work, but renounce its fruit. Be detached and work, but have no desire for work or reward.' It is a very challenging teaching, but its essence is totally liberating because when you can renounce the fruits of all actions you are free to act for its own sake and for love alone, to give of yourself without any need to get anything back. In simple terms our motto became 'God moves everything'.

Living from the core of non-attachment our greatest pleasure was to become a living Gita for each other. All the scriptures came alive for us. When someone read out the Sermon on the Mount one day we could immediately recognise its source as being the same as that of the Gita. Both were founded on truth. We discovered so much joy in not being bound by any one religion, embracing every faith, creed and philosophy in this way and recognising they really are all one.

As we knocked down walls and expanded the house we seemed to be making way for more people to join our community. Mansukh told us one weekend about someone who had come to his yoga class whom he felt was very special. 'She bounced in the door in the middle of the class and as soon as I saw her I got that familiar feeling that here was another person who was going to have a big part to play in our community.'

He was beaming from ear to ear as he told us about her. 'She is only tiny but her presence is enormous and greatly enhanced by a great mass of hair that almost explodes out from her head and matches her personality. I have never met anyone so exuberant and excited about being alive!' She'd obviously made quite an impression!

'I invited her to join us after the class for our usual evening socialising and she seemed very taken by the yoga. She's actually doing a degree in Physical Education at Bangor and is quite a gymnast. I think she is exploring yoga to try to calm her energy down a little bit.'

Her name was Annie and no sooner had he got used to this ball of energy than he discovered there were two of them! She had a twin sister called Jane who was studying drama down the coast at Aberystwyth. At Annie's recommendation she had started making the one hundred and twenty mile trip up to Bangor once a week just to come to yoga.

This dynamic duo, it seemed, were already famous all over Wales for their singing and we soon found out why. When they sang together it was like listening to angels and everywhere they went they had people in tears, including us. Little did Mansukh know at the time that Jane would later become his wife. Jane especially loved to sing songs from all spiritual traditions, and when she sang some of the ancient devotional songs that Mansukh's mother taught her it seemed as though she had always known them. The way she sang captivated us all, but especially Mansukh. Perhaps it was in that ancient space that their hearts met.

It wasn't long before Annie and Jane moved into Pinewood and brought a completely new and fresh energy into the community.

They came with Mansukh and others at weekends to help with the building work and when we saw Annie, at five foot nothing, picking up an angle grinder something told us that there was no limit to what she could do. And we were right. 'No limit' became another one of our mottoes. There was no limit to the possibilities of achieving our dream, because with the right people at the right time anything could be accomplished.

Annie and Jane

Life is a Curriculum

———————————— • ————————————

Relationships teach us what we need to learn

Some relationships can be very confronting because they often reflect the parts of us we don't like to admit to. The person at work we find so infuriating is showing us our own inner frustration so that we can find a way to resolve it. If, however, we reject and avoid the situation, we may have missed a golden opportunity to move beyond frustration.

Until we have developed a way to recognise and work with our own inner feelings there will always be people in life who behave in ways we find unacceptable or that spark off our own inner pain.

Relationships can be our greatest teachers in life

It's easy to say, 'I just can't handle it,' and keep running away. In fact, most people spend 70-80% of their energy manipulating events so as to successfully avoid feeling any discomfort with people or situations.

What this actually means is that we can miss more than half of our life and the valuable lessons we need to learn.

We can choose to learn from things or to simply ignore the lessons and blame other people for the way we feel. However, the wisest course of action is to work with the feelings people bring up in us, to enter into them and turn them towards our growth so that life can become a deeper, more meaningful experience for us.

Relationships can be our greatest teachers in life and when we can see them in this light they become an adventure into knowing ourselves.

114

Mansukh's brother, Umed, was a constant support to us and no job was too much for him. He threw himself into the building work with great gusto, being very capable and able to get jobs done quickly and efficiently. Ian, in contrast, was very slow and sure about the way he did things, taking great care to put all his love and concern into his work. I suppose it was inevitable that friction would occur sooner or later.

It happened over a small window that Ian was reclaiming. All the timber we used was second hand and he had spent literally weeks cleaning up the wood to make the window frame. Umed found this a bit much to cope with because he just wanted to get on with the job and get it finished. Every day he came back from work to see Ian lovingly caressing this exquisite window frame and in the end he just couldn't stand it any more. 'What are you doing with that damn window frame? You've been at it for weeks!' he shouted. And, of course, Ian reacted. Mansukh heard the angry exchange and hurried upstairs to see what was going on. He talked to them about the qualities that each one possessed and pointed out how very extraordinary they each were in their own special ways.

'Umed, you are always very caring towards people, and ready to give to anyone who needs help. Ian, you are very patient and considerate and never miss an opportunity to empower others. Both of you are very loyal and full of compassion. When we are in conflict we can only see the rough edges that we are rubbing up against and miss and forget all the beauty and the strength of the people involved. That is how the issue becomes bigger and more important than the people.'

This was his most important teaching to us all. 'People matter more than anything else. People matter more than getting the work done, more than achieving great things.' He asked them to express three things that they really admired about each other and before long they were both in tears and hugging each other. It was a beautiful process to watch and from that time on they were the best of friends.

Most of our disagreements were very short-lived because our common goal of wanting to live together harmoniously was more important to us than winning. Our rule of thumb was that yogis don't moan! Things were very difficult sometimes but to us it was all part of growing. We had to learn to compromise and have great respect for each other's opinions.

Pathways...

from Conflict to Freedom

◆ *Set yourself up for success*
Adopt a positive attitude like:
* 'This is an opportunity for me to grow and evolve towards my highest goal' or
* 'What fantastic outcome awaits me?'

◆ *Stay centred and grounded*
Stand in the middle of a conflict. If you stand in the middle of a boat it is balanced but if you go either to right or left the boat tips over. Focus on your heart centre.

◆ *Do not react*
Ninety nine percent of the things people express are not personal. By the time someone snaps at you it's usually a culmination of a hundred stresses and strains they've been under. Have a compassionate attitude to their predicament. Tell yourself that by not reacting you will bring greater growth and happiness into your life.

◆ *Separate yourself*
Visualise stepping aside from yourself so that people's behaviour is not affecting you.

◆ *Notice how you are breathing*
Holding the breath restricts your ability to stay centred, clear and creative. Breathe deeply!

◆ *Trust Yourself*
Know that you have survived much greater challenges. Remind yourself - you can handle anything.

Pathways ...

continued ...

◆ *Act now*
Have the expectation that something wonderful is going to happen.
Do not dwell on the conflict. Reverse the polarity by resolving it in
the moment.

◆ *Seek to listen first*
Rather than wanting to be listened to say, 'I'd like to solve this
problem with you but first I want to hear your story so I understand
what's important for you.' Few people will be able to resist this.
Listen to what the person is saying and not just with your ears. Use
your whole body to listen, giving them the space to fully express
their grievance without interruption.

◆ *What are their perceptions?*
You can be certain they are very different from yours! You need to
be able to understand or 'stand under' where other people are
coming from in order to be able to resolve a conflict.

◆ *Communicate your feelings*
Communicate in a way that is non-threatening, taking responsibility
for your own feelings without being over-forceful.

◆ *Respect and value the other person's feelings*
No matter how unreasonable people's ideas may be, whatever they
are expressing is their truth in that moment and they won't rest until
they are sure you understand and respect them.

◆ *Ace Card - try saying, 'You're right'*
It feels so good to let the other person win occasionally and it can do
more for your on-going relationship than almost anything else.

A monk was walking through the forest one day when a little monkey hit him on the head with a coconut.

He picked it up, broke it open and drank the milk inside it. After he had eaten the coconut to satisfy his hunger he used one half of the shell as a begging bowl.

If someone throws something at you, turn it into something that benefits you.

Chris' father was an expert carpenter and spent countless weekends helping Umed and Ian. He was one of those wonderful people who could fit in anywhere and with anyone and he and Dad became the best of friends even though they couldn't really understand each other's language. He loved Mum's bhajias - a special Indian delicacy - and he'd often say to Dad in his broad Liverpool accent, 'I'll have a few more budgies, Dad!'

Thakor, Mansukh's cousin, arrived just in time to move 'Mount Bilston', which was our name for the rubble that had accumulated in the garden. Thakor was a simple village boy from India, struggling to adapt to life in England and when he moved in he amazed everyone with the strength and power of his service. Whatever you asked him to do, whether it was cooking, cleaning or shovelling rubble, he did it with enthusiasm, efficiency and strength. He taught us all the essence of how to serve and today he has become the mainstay of the Life Foundation in India.

It took three of us ten hours nonstop work to fill three skips because we could only afford to hire the skips for one day. This was an example of the kind of energy we had and the pace we were moving at. Our 'no limit' motto meant that anything we set out to achieve became possible. The deadlines were important for us because they made us push ourselves to reach our goals, and we always made sure we were successful. It built a success consciousness that is still driving us today.

Working under this pressure inevitably brought about disputes and differences of opinion but we had an agreement to resolve them there and then and never to let any disagreement, however small, 'brew'. We also had a very positive attitude to conflict and saw it as something to propel us towards our own self-discovery.

'Think what fantastic outcome awaits you,' Mansukh told me once, 'because without challenges you will never discover yourself. They are a part of life that actually nurtures us in a deep way.'

'But sometimes people are so unreasonable,' I said.

'The most important thing with people,' he answered, 'is to try never to judge them. Let them be who they are and see them as agents for giving you a new dimension to your life. Turning every challenge or conflict to your advantage depends totally upon the attitude you hold towards it.

'Regardless of your age, maturity or health, conflict and challenges will always be a part of day to day living. Remember that they contain the opportunity to grow towards new levels of freedom.'

Right Understanding

•

Events are never good or bad in themselves, they just are

The negativity or positivity arises from the way we perceive what is happening. When our environment is distracting or agitating we simply need to have an enlightened attitude and a toolbox of skilful strategies that work.

In reality it's not easy to feel happy if someone does or says something that is confronting or painful, *but we do have a choice.* We can either go through life learning, growing and gaining from being with people or accumulating a huge backlog of hurts and resentments.

Right understanding helps us to look at a negative situation in a positive way

Right understanding helps us to look at a negative situation in a positive way, with gentleness and willingness, and to appreciate and remove the ignorance which prevents us from seeing situations *as they really are.*

What about people who are behaving badly?

The old Native American adage 'Don't judge a man till you've walked a mile in his moccasins' invites us to look deeper than the surface of people's behaviour. Everyone has pain inside them of one kind or another which affects their behaviour.

It's the easiest thing in the world to react to other people's negativity and therefore add to it but if you can ask yourself what they're really going through the answers can be very surprising.

P a t h w a y s ...

to Resolving Conflict

◆ *Focus on solutions*

    * Spend one tenth of your time on the problem and nine tenths of your time on answers.

    * Quickly write down the situation.

    * Then spend twice as long writing down all the ways you and they are going to benefit by solving this conflict.

    * Now spend nine times as long writing down solutions!
      Think of people who inspire you. What would they do?

    * Choose the best three solutions and act on them - now!

    * Respond and adapt. Carefully observe how well your ideas work in practice and be ready to flow and change until you find the best possible solution.

◆ *Deactivate the situation*
Replay the conflict situation over in your mind backwards, almost like rewinding a video. Do it several times, each time a little faster.

◆ *Visualise the other person involved*
See them as a cartoon character like Mickey Mouse. It will make you laugh and be more able to lighten up about the situation.

◆ *Remember*
You are never given anything that is too much for you to handle.

By now I had already been through so many personal barriers. Life had become a great adventure in self learning that provided me with a mirror to see myself in many different ways. I was in an environment that stretched me to my limits both physically and emotionally and at the same time offered me a wealth of insight into myself and my relationships with others. I was beginning to wonder what would come next on this vast evolutionary agenda and then, out of the blue, I received a letter from my old girlfriend.

The need for a close, secure relationship had always been very important to me but, as I had discovered, it demanded a huge investment of my energy. This was the one part of my life which I still felt unclear about and I needed clarity to understand the significance of relationships.

'What is your attitude to loving relationships, Mansukh?' I'd been meaning to ask this question for a long time.

He looked at me with more than a little mischief and asked, 'Having a bit of trouble, John?'

'Well.....,' I was hesitant to admit to this. 'I'm just curious really. It seems to be such a big area of struggle for so many people and you never seem to have any trouble with it.'

He grinned at me. 'Do you remember when I was in Manchester, John?'

'Yes, you were working that summer for a pharmaceutical company.'

'I was living in Eccles and a university friend turned up on my doorstep one day very keen to start a relationship with me. I knew that I didn't want to make a commitment that would restrict me in what I wanted to do in my life and I had to try to make that clear to her in the most sensitive way I could.

'It was quite tricky for a while so I invited her to come for a walk. It was late evening, I remember, as we walked through the streets of the town and we talked for hours about what it means to be committed to someone in a relationship. We ended up sitting on a bench outside the park under a canopy of trees in a very dark, deserted street about one in the morning when suddenly something extraordinary happened.

'A man appeared out of nowhere, running very fast towards a nine or ten foot wall which he scaled in seconds, closely followed by two policemen who found it much harder to get over. In fact, one of them had to heave the other up and over. They soon reappeared and were picked up by a police car, having failed to catch their quarry.

'I sat there wondering what it all meant and what were the implications

for the situation I was in at that moment. I knew that nothing ever happens by chance.

'It occurred to me that the first man going over the wall could be compared to the beginning of a relationship. Because it's something that we really want we inject a lot of enthusiasm and effort into it. The two policemen seemed to represent what happens after a while when we get complacent. We need each other's help to overcome the burdens of life. If one refuses to help then both are sunk.

'In any relationship there are a variety of forces at work and we need to continually inject fresh enthusiasm into it if we want it to work.

'A few minutes later we got up and walked away knowing that something had been resolved between us. That encounter led to a friendship that lasted for many years and made a big difference to both our lives. She was such a tremendous support and inspiration to me.

'So, in answer to your question, John, I think you have to be very clear in your life what you are looking for in a relationship.

'Create a relationship that doesn't bind or restrict you.'

Loving Relationships

—————————— • ——————————

Give all your love, not part

People often gravitate towards a relationship because they feel somehow incomplete on their own and are hoping that whatever they feel they are lacking will be fulfilled. Some people may feel the need to be loved or financially secure in order to feel whole while others may just be looking for someone to make them laugh.

People often find themselves caught up in a tangle of mortgages, children and all kinds of other things that they never bargained for, just because they wanted someone who could make them laugh or because they didn't want to feel lonely.

Everyone is really looking to feel complete, whole and fulfilled and the only way to really become fulfilled within a relationship is to give yourself to it with a one hundred percent unconditional commitment. This means that if you are wanting to feel love you will need to express your love without reservation.

People often say that they wish their partner would love them more, but if they are only expressing thirty percent of their love then that is all they will be feeling from their partner. The simple truth is that as soon as you give one hundred percent love to someone that is how much love you will feel. It's a boomerang effect.

> **If you are waiting
> for someone to love you -
> you could wait forever**

We all need to realise that we are our own source of love and that whatever we give comes straight back to us in a thousand different ways. If, however, you find yourself giving everything and feeling unfulfilled, it may be that you are giving unskilfully, perhaps with reservation, hesitation, judgement or expectation. Love needs to be unconditional. The moment you give with an expectation of return you are not truly giving.

124

P a t h w a y s . . .

to Perfect Relationships

Just like a new piano, your relationship needs constant tuning. Learn to respond skilfully to your partner so that the relationship doesn't become 'out of tune'.

Make a commitment to give 100% to the relationship to make it work.

Whenever you feel you need love - give love.

Be compassionate and understanding if your partner has an off day. Don't react or take it personally.

Make a pact to help to break each other's negative patterns. Your agreement may run something like this: 'If I lose my cool, please stick your tongue out or stand on your head to help me out of it!' This means that if your partner does something silly like getting angry you do something even *more* silly.

Never allow yourself to become complacent or to take your partner for granted. Always try to be as spontaneous and enthusiastic as you were when you first met. Surprise your partner with flowers or tickets to the theatre. Do anything that makes them feel special and always remember that predictability kills a relationship.

Express your love freely and often and never assume they know you love them.

Please remember you will only get the maximum out of your relationship if you trust it is going the right way, no matter what happens. If you are giving 100% of your love your effort of loving will inevitably lead you into a relationship that is fulfilling even if it isn't reciprocated.

Love one another, but make not a bond of love;
Let it rather be a moving sea between the shore
    of your souls.
Fill each other's cup but drink not from one cup.
Give one another of your bread but eat not
    from the same loaf;
Sing and dance together and be joyous,
    but let each of you be alone,
Even as the strings of a lute are alone
    though they quiver with the same music.
Give your hearts, but not into each other's
    keeping.
For only the hand of Life can contain your
    hearts.
And stand together yet not too near together:
For the pillars of the temple stand apart,
And the oak tree and the cypress grow not in
    each other's shadow.

Kahlil Gibran

Jane and Mansukh

The Life Foundation in Bosnia - Eurowalk 2000

Unconditional Love

I thought of Mum and Dad and what it was about their relationship that was so special. Was it the mutual respect they had for each other or the fact that they had never stopped expressing their love for one another? Each one knew they had a unique contribution to make to the relationship and because they lived by the spiritual laws they never doubted that providence was always working for them, no matter what happened. This meant that they trusted the relationship would always work out.

The most compelling thing about them is that they were each content in themselves so that they were never looking to each other for their contentment. In fact, they were only ever looking for what they could give to the other and never craved physical comfort or emotional replenishment. They each had realised that the reason they came together was to help the other to reach their spiritual goal and to remind each other to always turn towards the source and the light. This silent agreement created such a deep bond between them that nothing could ever break it.

How often I watched them walking along the road together, or cooking or singing together in our group, or chasing each other up the stairs and realised that they had a real friendship made in heaven.

I always think of them as friends, not just to each other but to me also. For as long as I can remember my relationship with them has been one of equal understanding and listening. They looked on me as an equal and never a junior. They respected my views and perceptions and made time to listen to me and where I was coming from.

They never taught me by harsh discipline but through fun. Mum always invited me to join her in whatever she was doing, so I would sit and help her to pick grit out of the moong beans when she could easily have sent me out to play.

Their Gandhian upbringing made them incredibly patient and tolerant, probably much more so than most parents. They always lived by Gandhi's principles of 'simple living, high thinking' and had a positive regard for life. They lived within an ambience of unconditional love and perhaps that is the secret for their immense triumph over the tragedies that beset their lives. They would always be positive and laugh even if things were really bad. And when they had their differences it was always in good humour because they both had a total assurance that, no matter what happened, they would never withdraw their love from each other.

Mansukh

Unconditional Love

———————————— • ————————————

Love is the only healer

Unconditional love is a free expression of love that emerges when we can let go of our attachment to and desperation for end results. This not only applies to practical things like achieving our goals but to wanting things like love.

When we are not emotionally attached to our doing and being, life is allowed to take its own course. We find we are not interfering or trying to make things happen.

> **Unconditional love accepts all things as they are**

Pooh Bear is probably the best example of this way of being! Pooh, in his wisdom, recognises the perfection of each moment and just flows along with things as they present themselves to him. His uncomplicated and accepting philosophy is simply 'Pooh Is'. In a nutshell, unconditional love accepts all things as they are.

It's not easy to do, however, as we have all been conditioned to 'achieve' and to try to manipulate people and events in order to 'get things done'. Flowing in the moment like Pooh Bear may not seem the most attractive proposition to the western mind, but that is precisely why people are full of anxiety and stress in this modern world. The mind is on overdrive.

We have to retrain ourselves to stop rushing and to slow down enough to taste the flavour of this moment. Be very patient with yourself, though. You cannot expect to achieve this state overnight. Whenever you try to touch unconditional love in your life please remember to approach it with joy and lightness, as if your life depended on it.

131

Pathways...

to Magic Moments

◆ ***Strength comes from letting go***
Unconditional love is the quintessence of creativity and is always full
of surprises! If you want to fill your life with magic moments be
willing to:
* Relax your expectations. Unconditional love will make things
  turn out even better.
* Let go of fixed ideas. Unconditional love will give you better
  ones.
* Let go of wanting something in return. You'll end up receiving
  more than you ever expected.

◆ ***Magic moments - the power of unconditional love***
If you are with someone and want to know how to create a moment
of magic with them use your heart power.

* Sit in a comfortable place, close your eyes and relax.

* Shift awareness to your heart space by relaxing your thoughts and
  focusing on the region behind your sternum (see page 29).

* Activate your heart power by thinking of someone you love and
  respect very dearly - a child, a close friend, someone who has
  helped you very much. Send sincere feelings of love and
  appreciation to them and to yourself.

* Now, think of the person you are with and silently ask the
  question, 'What can I do now that will make life special for this
  person?'

* Listen deeply - ***and then act*** on the ideas that come. Trust and be
  brave. The results are always worth it!

I found myself thinking about how far we had all come together and the commitment we had made to each other. How had it happened? And what was the main ingredient that made it work? And then it hit me.

The thing that had catalysed our coming together and staying together was, quite simply, love. Unconditional love. The underlying force behind it all had been that we had all met someone who knew how to love people unconditionally, without any reservation or judgement and for no apparent reason. Whenever we were with him or his parents we felt embraced by this quality of love and it had allowed the very best to come out of us. When you feel loved and accepted in this way you no longer have to prove yourself. You can just be who you are and, within that, find your own strengths and talents.

I remember the time Chris told Mansukh he was about to be thrown out of university. 'Why is that, Chris?' he asked him. 'I haven't done any work,' Chris replied. 'I've been going out to parties and pubs every night.'

'Well, you know what to do, Chris,' Mansukh said gently, without any trace of judgement.

That day Chris asked himself what it was he had to do. All of a sudden the answer came to him. If he wanted to stay at university he would have to stop doing all the things that were distracting him. Overnight he gave up alcohol, meat and anything else he could think of that wasn't good for him! Interestingly, he lost all his friends overnight as well, but he didn't seem to mind.

Mansukh then invited him to study in the library with him every day, and for two weeks they went in at nine o'clock in the morning and didn't come out until 5 o'clock at night.

'There was something about studying with him on one side of the table and me on the other,' he told me, 'that made it somehow easy to learn. He hadn't judged me in any way but just offered his unconditional support to help me to get through my exams. And from a fat row of zeros I got through easily.'

When I think of Mum and Dad their lives were a total expression of this kind of love. They had accepted us all into their home, feeding sometimes ten to fifteen people they didn't even know at the drop of a hat. They even gave up their bed for us.

When the group first converged on their home in Bilston there wasn't enough room for everyone to sleep. Without hesitation they gave up their bedroom and threw out the bed to make space for everyone. The bed was buried in the garden, but that is another story that cannot be told here! Two old people sacrificed their comfort so that we could evolve spiritually. How many parents would do that?

We had all been learning an unconditional way of being with each other over the years and now we had to learn how to become as unconditional with the rest of the world.

'But sometimes people are exasperating, Mansukh! How can you be unconditional with them?' I was finding out that it was one thing to love people that it was easy to get on with, but very hard with people I disagreed with.

'Try not to judge people, John,' he said, 'and accept them as they are. Judgement stops us from seeing the real beauty of a person and the larger picture.......'

Dad

Expanding the Frame

———————————— • ————————————

Seeing life in an unlimited way

Imagine owning a huge Leonardo da Vinci canvas. If you were to only frame one small corner of it and say, 'This is it, it's not very interesting,' people would call you insane.

But our lives are a masterpiece that we treat in this way. We judge ourselves and each other in such a way that it limits the true picture of who we are down to one fuzzy little corner. When we can move beyond judgement and prejudice and into an unconditional attitude we are essentially expanding the frame and therefore can begin to glimpse the greater picture.

Our lives are a masterpiece

Judgement locks us into a space where we can only see our own point of view with a total conviction that we are 'right' and they are 'wrong'. This creates a cage around us through which we are unable to see that, in fact, everyone is perfect as they are. Everyone has a perfect plan for their life and is moving along just as they should be, like everything else in creation. No-one is right or wrong. We are all just doing the best we can with what is in front of us.

Once we are able to accept ourselves unconditionally we will find we are able to extend that same attitude towards others and free ourselves from the cage of righteousness. We become free to see that everyone is perfect as they are *no matter what they have done* and to simply *let them be.* You can dislike the sin while you try never to hate the sinner.

This is not to say, however, that we do not have a responsibility to create harmony around us.

135

During a meditation retreat one of the students was caught stealing. It was immediately reported to the main teacher with the request that the culprit be thrown out. The teacher chose to ignore it and when the student was caught stealing yet again, he disregarded the incident in the same way.

The other students were furious and threatened to leave en masse if the thief was not dealt with. The teacher gathered all his students together. He told them that they were wise enough to know right from wrong and they could go somewhere else to study if they wanted to. Because the thief didn't yet know right from wrong he intended to keep him there so that he could teach him, even if everyone else left.

The thief was moved to tears by the teacher's attitude and compassion and never stole again.

Pathways...

to Expanding the Frame

◆ *Imagine*

* Can you imagine accepting people exactly as they are, allowing them to be who they are, doing what they are doing in whatever way they choose to do it?

* Can you imagine feeling compassion for people who hurt you, being able to see their actions as separate from them?

* Can you imagine being in a space of non-judgement with an attitude of total respect for each person and where they are in life - no matter who they are or what they have done?

* Can you imagine having the courage to allow people to make their own mistakes, trusting in their own process?

* Can you imagine standing firm by truth and intervening to prevent conflict or disharmony without reacting aggressively?

If you can imagine it - you can do it!

◆ *Expand the frame*

Make a list of everything you value in the people around you.
* How do they add to your life?
* How do they give strength, support and value to people around them?

When you are with people ask yourself quality questions like:
* 'What can I learn from them?
* 'What incredible outcome could arise from being with this person?'

'When you can accept everyone as they are,' Mansukh continued, 'it opens a doorway to a whole new experience of relationships, because essentially we expand out of our separateness and into the oneness of everything.

'I never put anyone out of my heart, no matter what they have done, because I always remind myself that the person in front of me is just like me, with the same yearnings that I have, to be loved and valued. They are capable of suffering the same pain of rejection and judgement.

'This is the kind of attitude that enables people like Mother Teresa to treat the people she finds dying in the street as if they were her own relatives. Instead of condemning the old man in the gutter with wounds full of maggots for being in such a terrible state, she sees him as someone who is evolving in his own way. She does everything she can to assist that process, be it towards recovery or simply dying with dignity.

'Cultivate attitudes of acceptance, tolerance and forgiveness, John,' he said, 'and then you are giving people the space to change instead of empowering their faults.

'But you know, John, unconditional love is far more than a warm feeling for someone. It is about vital, creative actions that meet people's true needs. Gandhi said that the way God showed himself to the poor and hungry of India was in the form of work, clothing and food. Love has to be practical actions that bring about greater harmony, well-being and happiness in people's lives. You have to be able to listen carefully to what is needed in people. You need to listen deeply, silently, unconditionally, in such a way that the person feels empowered by your listening. You have to listen so deeply to people that they enjoy your listening.

'Become delighted at the experience of listening.......'

Listening

●

Listening is the activity of the heart

In the art of communication, listening is the most powerful skill of all. Most people don't know how to listen because we are trained to be outspoken and to get our point across. We learn to put all our energy into being heard and making others understand us rather than trying to understand them.

I truly believe that partial listening is responsible for eighty or ninety percent of the rifts that occur between people. So often our communications are competitive with both parties determined to 'win'. Wouldn't it make a refreshing change to let the other person win? If they win and it makes us happy then we have both won.

It is the quality of your listening that transforms others

What we don't realise is that in becoming a listener, fully engaged in listening, one of the most powerful forces for healing is set free. It not only enriches others' lives to be heard but it helps us to understand others more deeply. This of course, enriches our own life.

The greatest achievements of my life began with being willing to listen in even the smallest exchange. Ideas were sparked off that led me towards everything I have ever done. For instance, if I had not been willing to listen to my father's casual remarks on one particular day I might never have begun the world peace journey that took us to thirty one countries and into the lives of hundreds of people.

Give yourself the opportunity to listen to what people have to say

Listen in such a way that everything is calm and still. Listen with an attitude of gentle acceptance. Each word is then heard with its true meaning. The listener and the speaker become one and a beautiful melody and dance begin between you.

139

There was once a brilliant violinist. He was
in great demand, giving concerts all over
the world. His brother accompanied him
wherever he went and could always be seen
sitting right at the front of the concert hall
in rapt attention.

As soon as his brother started to play, he
went into an ecstasy, listening so deeply
that he was completely oblivious to
anything else around him.

When his brother died the violinist threw
his violin on the funeral pyre with him.
Thinking he must be distraught with grief,
the shocked onlookers reproached him for
his rash action. His response was quite
simple. 'My violin is useless to me without
the depth of my brother's listening.'

Pathways...

to the Power of Listening

◆ *Learn to listen to yourself*

At least three times a day pause for a moment's reflection.

* Sit or stand comfortably and calm the racing mind with deep, relaxing breaths.
* Listen to the sounds of your own body - the rustling of clothing, your breath or your heartbeat.
* Become an observer of the sounds around you. Let them wash over you without thinking about them.
* After a few minutes of listening ask yourself:

    'What can I do now to feel better?'

    'What can I do that will help at least one person around me?'
* Take *immediate action* on the ideas that come.

◆ *The power of unconditional listening*

Devote some of the time you are with people to 'total listening':

* Listen to their words as if your life depended on it.
* Listen with your heart. What is their deepest intention? How are they hoping to heal, grow or gain in happiness as a result of talking with you?
* Refrain from giving your point of view. Simply try to find out everything you can about *their* reality.
* Give people the space to bless you instead of empowering their faults.

How would you like to be listened to? Listen like this yourself and watch how your listening heals others.

Bardsey Island Retreat

*Unity
and
Oneness*

As soon as I finished my doctorate I was free to go to India. My parents had left the little village of Sarav in the state of Gujerat in their early twenties to live in Kenya and it had always been my burning ambition to take them 'home'.

Our community was very strong by now and I was confident that everyone was established enough to continue to flourish. I was hoping to explore and investigate the ancient teachings of India and to bring them back to enrich our lives even more. We spent nine months in India, during four of which I toured around with Swami Dayananda, a master of Vedanta and a very charismatic teacher.

I learned everything I could from him that would help us to deepen our practice of spirituality, learning self reliance and discipline which brought a new, brighter and more focused spirit into our lives. I found myself plunged into a deeper prayer, seeking a greater strength to make our youthful energy more available to serve people.

We were discovering that perfect friendship really does cast out all of our superfluous differences, although very slowly. We were gradually learning to become one soul, one body, living and breathing as a group and no longer separate. As we became free from our own biased needs the principle of oneness was beginning to really come alive for us and our actions become more valid.

An untouchable force and power of love had been directing us. This force guides all people, everywhere, whether they are aware of it or not and our purpose was to find more ways to engage in such a communion.

As we applied ourselves more and more to the service of others we slowly learned that we need never 'worry' at any level about our future. Our faith in the power that was moving through us was growing in leaps and bounds and we got a tremendous joy out of others being equally important, and sometimes more important, than we were.

The greatest lesson of Maristowe for everyone was the power of service. It proved to me once and for all that if you focus on serving others without complication of your personal needs then, quite simply, heaven comes to earth. We were hardly even aware of our own needs after a while and 'hoarding' was unknown. We each tried to keep only what we immediately needed for the day and slowly selfishness and separateness were dying and our hearts were beginning to grow towards true unity.

Mansukh

Friendship - the First Step to....

The heart of friendship lies within the recognition that we are all one

True friendship is one of the most precious things in life. When you have true friends it is a divine and beautiful thing.

Many soldiers come back from the army remembering the times of friendship and support through danger and difficulty more than the perils they encountered. Why? Because in friendship we encounter an unconditional support, humour and opportunity to do more exciting and deeper things in life than we would be able or brave enough to do on our own.

An attitude of giving makes friendship work

If we remain isolated from other people no amount of wealth or knowledge can fulfil us, because without friendship life cannot really have any meaning or purpose. Friendship feels so natural to us, but what we must realise is that it doesn't just happen passively. We have to participate in it.

We need to calm the mind so it has space for friends, for an agitated mind doesn't have time for people. A mind that is content seems to find unlimited love and energy for everyone who comes along. If we can't love our friends in this way, can life really have any true meaning or purpose?

When you really express friendship you have to love. This means stepping out of yourself and giving. We need to give in order to form a creative, flowing exchange between ourselves and other people.

It is an attitude of giving that makes friendship work and when we can put as much energy, time and effort into giving as we do into trying to receive, something very beautiful begins to happen.

145

Amidst some of the worst violence in South Africa in the early 1990s Nelson Mandela received a unique visit in his prison cell. It was President F.W. de Klerk. Over the next two hours the two men talked alone while their supporters fought each other across the country. De Klerk shared his opinion that their nation had reached a moment in time where peace might just be possible. Together they explored the issues they felt were important, each attempting to sense the genuineness of the other. In de Klerk's words 'we both concluded in that meeting that here was a man I could do business with'.

At the end of their meeting the two men shook hands.

From that moment on, the image of that handshake was beamed across South Africa. It became a symbol of hope that held up even when the developing peace negotiations seemed most hopeless. The two leaders developed a working relationship where they could always phone each other and discuss issues even amidst boycotts and walkouts.

Their gesture of friendship, reinforced at every opportunity, was often a great risk to their lives and their reputations. Yet their handshake became one of the central rocks upon which South African society ended apartheid and started the long road to unity.

Friendship often requires risks but it is always worth it. It is the first step towards unity.

Pathways...

to Building Friendships

◆ *Give your mind space for others*
* Spend a few moments in quiet every day, especially whenever you start to feel 'busy'. Use some of the Pathways from Chapter Two to build a reservoir of calm so you have time for the people around you.

◆ *When you meet people*
Before you say anything to the people you meet:
* Think of them as human beings, with joys, loves and sorrows just like you.
* Empathise what they might be feeling right now.
* Ask yourself how you can help them expand their joys and heal their sorrows.
* Now begin your conversation with them.

◆ *Keys to creating friendship*
* Before you go to sleep at night think of one of your friends.
* Be grateful for all they give to you.
* Think of one thing you could do to add something special to their life:- give them a gift, make them laugh, massage their shoulders when they're stressed, surprise them with something they really value.
* Find a way to act on your idea the very next day.

◆ *Look, laugh, listen*
* Look for ways you can give to your friends' lives.
* Cultivate lightness, humour and a sense of fun in your friendships.
* Listen for their deeper needs. Offer a listening ear or a shoulder to lean on in times of crisis. Throw a surprise party for them.

By now our spiritual life had become a tapestry of disciplines interspersed with teachings, building work, prayer and service to the community. Now it was time to develop our skills as teachers. Maristowe was only half built but we had to combine our activities even more skilfully.

Just as Mansukh was leaving for India he threw Annie, Jane and Rita into confusion by asking them to take over all his classes in Bangor. They had never taught yoga or meditation before, but he was quite confident they would have no problem at all. As we waited in the airport lounge for their flight, which was delayed for three or four hours, Mansukh taught us all the importance of relaxation in yoga.

Somehow they missed the plane! Like everything else in our lives it was perfect. It meant we had to stay in London together for another twenty four hours and one of our friends who had come to see them off offered his house to us for the night. We didn't sleep a wink because Mansukh took this golden opportunity to teach us how to make yoga classes effective. I don't know why, but I have always found that the most significant and important teachings seem to be given in the most relaxed way at times when you are completely exhausted!

While he was away, we realised how strong we had become as a group. It was also a test of putting everything we had learned into practice. We found that we cared enough about each other to overcome any differences of opinion and it proved to us that we were going to stay together no matter what. We were beginning to really feel the power of true friendship in our lives and how much it meant to us.

Friendship is commitment to each other and giving each other the space to be who you are. Through all the trials that came to meet us it was the power of our friendship that really helped us to survive. We also had a strong vision that if we could make a community work, then the possibility of it happening on a grander scale, in the world, would be much, much greater.

Although we all went out of our way to create harmony in every interaction it was not always easy to achieve. While it may be part of human nature to disagree, our joint vision was greater than our desire to win or be 'right'. The beauty of living together was that although we may have had many judgements about each other, for many different reasons, we were quick to let go of them. We knew that every interaction had an effect on the world at large and that it was more important to help to

create global harmony than to win a dispute.

We also had some incredible tools to help us, mainly the Aarati, Mum and Dad's chappatis, and the many visiting swamis who always seemed to turn up at the right moment. This created so much strength within the group that by the time Mansukh came back from India we were all completely sure that 'Life' was here to stay.

His return marked the beginning of a new phase of intensive learning. The building work on Maristowe was completed and we settled down to study what Mansukh had learned in India. We entered into a period of intense spiritual focus which, in fact, constituted the very first Dru Yoga Diploma Course. We were to be the first people to learn the principles of Dru Yoga in a concrete way, from teaching skills, anatomy and physiology to the highest Upanishadic truths. We studied every morning from six till eight before work and every evening until about midnight. Weekends were intense! This involved non-stop practice and absorption, going deeply into postures and developing new therapies as well as delving into Vipassana meditation and Vedantic philosophy. This knowledge became the solid foundation from which we were to springboard ourselves into serving the world.

'We have been invited to sing at the Buddhist centre in Birmingham tomorrow.' Mansukh had just received an invitation on the phone. We had become quite famous locally for our singing, having built up a repertoire of inspirational songs from all traditions, singing in many different languages including English, Sanskrit and Latin. Every night Bilston rocked (and still does) to the sound of our singing which had become a major source of inspiration and energy for us all. We had become a bit of a novelty amongst the Asian communities as a mainly English group of people who could sing songs in their language. Now we were off to Birmingham and this turned out to be a very important day for us.

It was here that we first met the Reverend Terasawa, who at that time was a senior monk in the Myohoji Nipponzan Buddhist order. He was very striking to look at with a powerful sense of presence.

He was the last speaker that day and when he stood up and started talking we were all riveted. 'It's all very well talking about peace,' he said, 'but really you have to go out and do something.' I noticed Mansukh listening acutely. 'You have to make a stand for peace,' he continued. 'It's not good enough to just sit and meditate.' He then talked about how his order, the

Nipponzan Myohoji, walk their talk, fearlessly entering into war zones, meeting people, making sure they make an impact on the world.

Mansukh couldn't wait to meet him and immediately invited him to come to Maristowe the very next day to talk with us, which he did. As soon as he arrived, dressed in his beautiful white and saffron robes, we knew we had someone very special in our midst. He talked to us about his work as a peace maker and showed us his famous finger, half of which he had burned away as a demonstration of his commitment to peace. He also told us about the Peace Pagoda that he had commissioned to be built in Battersea Park to mark the one hundredth anniversary of their teacher, Fuji Guru. They needed help to get the Pagoda built and without hesitation we offered our services.

We travelled up to London for a few days at a time and lived with sixty monks in a big metal shack. At four in the morning a big bell rocketed us out of our sleeping bags and we followed the rush of bodies out of the door. The next thing we knew we were being blasted with freezing cold water from a hose pipe skilfully wielded by one of the monks. Swish! Swish! And you were done. At weekends there were often more than eighty of us lined up together. It made you very alert and alive to the moment!

We joined in their prayers at six o'clock, had breakfast at seven thirty and then worked non-stop all day on the scaffolding. It was freezing cold with snow on the ground and the work was exhausting (although this was not an unfamiliar experience), but it felt so good to be working together with other people with such a great sense of purpose.

Rev. Nagase, Nipponzan Order

Life team - Battersea Park Peace Pagoda, London

Unity

———————————— • ————————————

What is the Purpose of Life?

This is a big question, and one that actually contains within itself everything that you are, everything you believe you are, and everything you would like to become.

In fact this is the very question that drives each one of us to work so hard every day, to invest so much time, effort and planning into accumulating and disposing of wealth and possessions to try to give purpose to our life.

> **The purpose of life is to create unity in everything we do and with everyone we meet**

If you ever feel lonely, isolated, confused or unhappy it's possible that you haven't searched deeply enough for the answer to this question. If your life has gone by very rapidly and the last ten to sixty years have just drifted past, then perhaps you have not stayed still long enough to really discover the purpose of your life.

People like to believe that life is about being separate and isolated from one another. But when separation is our foundation in life it creates so many problems for us, simply because it isn't *true*. We are all connected to one another and to every living thing, every animal, bird and creature, every blade of grass, every flower and drop of rain.

When we feel separate it creates a sense of fear in us, for one stick on its own is weak and can be broken. We may try to feel strength through manipulation, exploitation, accumulation and having power over others. But real strength lies in unity. If you put twenty sticks together they can never be broken.

152

Pathways...

to Unity in Your Life

◆ *Write these questions on your bathroom mirror*
* What is the purpose of my life?
* Where is my life going?
* What am I going to do to make the rest of my life incredible?

◆ *Write these questions on the dashboard of your car:*
* Where is my life going?
* Why am I travelling in this car?

The deeper your reasons become, the greater will be the strength and power of your journey.

◆ *Creating unity*
Try this, just for a month:
* Every time you get angry with someone, give £10 away to someone.
* Every time you meet someone you don't like, give them a gift.

This is not suppression, it is transformation. Within a few days, you'll discover an irrepressible power that when allowed to blossom can affect thousands.

◆ *Compliment people*
* Every time you want to condemn someone, compliment them instead.
* Every time you meet someone you don't like, give them a compliment.

Complimenting people puts your mind on a different tangent. Try something like 'You're looking well' or 'That's a great jacket.'

What a glorious sight! A hundred and twenty monks and nuns from various orders all assembled together with their shaven heads and flowing robes in different shades of saffron and orange. There seemed to be a pool of stillness around them as they waited in silence for the prayers to begin. A large percentage were Christian as well as the Buddhist orders, joined by Hindus, Jews, Zoroastrians and, in fact, just about every faith you can imagine. They represented a great wealth of spiritual traditions coming together in a quite unprecedented way.

We were about to start the Nipponzan peace walk from Canterbury to London to commission the opening of the Peace Pagoda. It had always been Fuji Guru's vision to have a Peace Pagoda in London and an interfaith walk to commission its opening and here we were, a witness to the power of that vision.

Each group offered a prayer from their own faith before the walk began and it created such a beautiful atmosphere of bonding and unity. It was also a very emotional moment for me as I could sense the power of the spiritual energy that is naturally generated when we forget our differences and share our commonness. It felt so right to be worshipping in so many different ways and languages, all together as one humanity, each one sharing a deep respect for the others' faiths. In that moment I felt so glad to be alive and a part of something that was crossing the boundaries that separate human beings. As I reflected that most of the wars and the killing we have seen on this earth have been caused by man's inability to accept another man's God, my mind flashed back to the mountain top all those years ago. I recaptured that moment when I'd given my life to serve the world. As I stood watching and feeling the power of our unity I could feel my heart's longing for the killing and wars to stop. Mansukh's words were ringing in my ears, 'the purpose of your life is to create unity...' I could sense my father was there with me, feeling the strength of this moment, sharing the depth of my own longing for a united humanity.

We walked out of Canterbury with the Nipponzan monks leading the way, beating their traditional drums and chanting their call to peace, 'Na-Mu-Myo-Ho-Ren-Ge-Kyo'. Their huge purple peace banner flew above them heralding their purpose and strength. The vision of this march often took my breath away. Like the sight of the long procession of monks and nuns in their orange and white robes crossing a field of rape in full bloom. They looked magnificent and regal amidst the blaze of iridescent yellow.

Unity in Action

A flock of geese in flight is one of the most beautiful sights. The way they fly together is a perfect depiction of unity.

There is a sense of a common purpose about them as the first goose breaks the current of air and takes the impact, enabling the others to work less hard. After two or three miles another goose takes the lead and in this way they are able to fly for hundreds of miles together.

Imagine what would happen up there in the sky if even *one* of them refused to co-operate. It is clear to see that co-operation is a prerequisite for unity and a common cause. The geese are all helping each other to get to their destination.

What is our destination?

What is the common cause that we are all here to achieve?

The Loneliness of Separation

When we can create unity in our lives we touch the oneness of life

Bringing unity into our lives and into this world takes more than one person. We were made to be with others. It is the way it is meant to be. That is why joining up with other people creates such a beautiful feeling within us and simply feels 'right'.

Become willing to participate with people

Imagine for a moment that you are an iceberg, a massive, frozen entity, suspended by infinite volumes of water. Imagine the loneliness you feel as you float icebound and separate, unable to move. Imagine the longing you feel to simply melt into the ocean.

We are like this when we stubbornly refuse to acknowledge the oneness of life and cling instead to the belief that we are all alone and separate in a hostile world.

The iceberg only has to become warmer in order to become one with the ocean. In the same way, we need to melt the barriers of separation we have created in order to experience our unity and oneness.

Loneliness, isolation and separation never feel right, so the challenge we have in bringing peace and harmony into our lives and into this world is to become *willing* to participate with people and events around us.

Bringing unity into our life and into this world takes more than one person

157

Pathways...

from Separation to Unity

◆ *These things create separation*

> Gossiping about other people
> Judging others harshly or unnecessarily
> Competitiveness and trying to feel better than others
> Power seeking and cutting others down
> Hiding away in isolation

These things create unity

> Empowering others
> Non-judgemental attitudes and acceptance
> Selfless actions
> Concern for others
> Generosity

The choice is yours.

◆ *Watch your thoughts*

* Ask yourself:
Do my thoughts create oneness or separation?
Do my thoughts create love or hatred?
Do my thoughts create trust or mistrust?

Remember, your thoughts create your world. You can use techniques like Introspection (page 74) to create new habits of positive, successful and harmonising ways of relating to others.

'You are leading the walk today, John.' Mansukh had that big smile on his face as he told me. 'No problem,' I said, feeling confident that God was on my side. What I didn't know was that God was planning to use the opportunity to play with me. At one stage the walk went through the fairly thick and undifferentiated forest on one of the Downs and for some reason there was a Japanese film crew running up and down trying to film us. Somehow or other Mansukh became distracted by the film crew and disappeared, leaving me to march ahead with one hundred and twenty monks and nuns striding behind me, chanting and beating their drums, full of trust in their leader. As fate would have it, somewhere in the forest I took a left turn when I should have turned right. After about ten minutes I began to get a particularly uncomfortable feeling that things weren't quite as they should be. It is not an easy thing to turn a peace walk around and march it back in the same direction, so I found myself racking my brains as to how to go about it without losing too much face.

Then I hit upon a plan. As soon as we got to the point where I was completely sure we had, in fact, gone wrong I called a kind of break. This meant that everybody had to sit down. Things might have gone smoothly from this point had it not been for the fact that the local resident there had a field full of thoroughbred horses and the monks' drums had upset them. The owner came charging out with his big hounds. 'How dare you come down here, singing and banging drums across my land?' he shouted. That was all I needed. Here I was, trying desperately to gather my composure so that I could nonchalantly ask everybody to walk back up the hill again, as if I had deliberately brought them down for a tea break, and here was this extremely irate person demanding retribution.

Luckily, Mansukh arrived on the scene at this moment to lend his support and together we managed to calm him down.

'What are you doing down here?' his eyes were saying to me as we started to march up the hill to get back onto the path. I just smiled at him and fixed my eyes on the road ahead in a glazed kind of way. Nobody knew what I went through that day and I am still not sure if they swallowed the story that we had just gone a mile out of our way for a tea break.

Unity & Oneness

---•---

Lack of unity is the disease of humanity

A leaf having fallen from the tree, trodden on and whisked around by the wind: how does it know it is part of the oak? It is the oak.
We are like this when we have no association with the greatness of our life and our connection to the universe.

> **Love is the most common expression of oneness**

When we can create unity in our lives we touch the oneness of life.
Oneness is another name for love, friendship and trust and these are some of the very foundation stones for a global family.

The oneness of life gives us the qualities of freedom and all-embracing love which can totally remove the existence of fear in our lives. Love is the most common expression of oneness. Everyone understands love because it is universal and natural to us all, as are other human values like goodness, honesty and non-violence that exist inherently within every culture. Love creates harmony, bringing people together by its very nature. Hatred creates disharmony and fragmentation, separating one human being from another.

So if you want to realise your purpose in life, to create unity and experience the oneness of all things, begin by allowing your thoughts to create peace and love, acknowledging your connection to everything and having respect and compassion for all beings.

In fact, the single most important factor is having compassion, for when that is present in our every thought, word and deed, it will automatically bring oneness.

> **Generosity connects us to the oneness of life**

LOVE CREATES HARMONY

P a t h w a y s ...

to Experiencing Oneness

◆ **Sounds create unity**
Sound connects us to every other vibration in life.
* Sing a simple vowel sound like Ooh. Relax the throat and sustain the note for the length of your breath.
* Breathe in and repeat the sound - not too loud, not too soft.
* Feel the stillness that follows just before your in-breath.
* Try different sounds like Aw, Aah, Ee.

◆ **Generosity instantly connects you to oneness**
Think of a time when you have given to someone - and it has been *exactly* what they needed. Recall the special feeling of warmth, lightness and fullness you felt as a result. This is the feeling of oneness!
* Find ways to surprise people with gifts or offers of help.
* Give without anybody knowing. Try this with your friends and watch how you feel afterwards.

◆ **Gratitude - the attitude for success**
Gratitude brings acceptance, freedom from struggle and removes resistance. Openly express gratitude for every trial and challenge in your life as well as for all the good things. Every morning before you get out of bed, say:
* Three things I am grateful for are ...
* Three people I am grateful for are ...
* Three challenges I am grateful for are ...

'Can you cook for three hundred people and bring it to us by tomorrow lunch time?' Mansukh was on the phone to Rita in Maristowe.

'Of course!' Rita was full of confidence. By now we were always ready to take on any new situation and sure enough Rita, Umed and Pushpa, Umed's wife, threw themselves into action working all night to prepare the food. We were responsible for all the cooking and cleaning on the walk, as well as helping everybody in any way we could. On this particular day the place we had arranged for accommodation didn't have any cooking facilities. Every challenge became another opportunity to explore different ways to give, to share and to serve with passion. Walking with the monks clearly showed us that the greater our intention to serve others the more joy we felt and the more we realised that real happiness lies in actively giving to others.

As the week went by we built up a great rapport with the monks and in the evening after prayers there was such an atmosphere of peaceful togetherness. Often the young Japanese monks gave Shiatsu to the older ones, while quite a lot of dialogue built up between the groups. The Theravadan Buddhists were mostly western monks in an eastern order and got on particularly well with the Japanese monks, although they were very different in their ways. The Theravadans are a contemplative order and carry a deep, still presence around them whereas the Japanese monks are very lively, active karma yogis. They are always serving and giving in a very one-pointed way that leaves no slackness in their day. They both gave me very powerful insights and impressions of how a seeker should be.

On the final day we walked into Battersea. This was a very special occasion because monks from all over the world had come to join us. By the time we had walked past the end of Downing Street the number of monks had swollen to nearly five hundred and the feeling was quite incredible as we walked to Westminster Abbey and the Cathedral, where Cardinal Hulme was waiting to receive the walkers on the steps. We made a magnificent sight. A pure vision of unity in action.

Umed and Pushpa

There was once a beautiful golden songbird. Every song he sang was always new and different and contained the sweetest sounds you could ever wish to hear. He lived in the forest with many other songbirds who loved and respected him for his wisdom and creativity.

One day a hunter came to the woods during the night and placed a net under the tree where the songbirds lived, laying seeds on the ground to trap them. In the morning the beautiful birds came down to pick at the seeds and the golden songbird immediately flew down to warn them to fly away because he could sense there was danger.

Before he could get to them the hunter closed the net around them and they were trapped. All the birds panicked except the golden songbird, who just started to sing a beautiful song. He sang so beautifully that all the other birds began to join in. This calmed them down and then the golden songbird told them that if they could gently flap their wings as well as they had been able to sing they would become free. As they did so the net lifted into the air, to the utter amazement of the hunter who could only stand by in awe and respect at the power of their unity.

'There are so many wars going on around the world, Dad, I find it very disturbing.' My father and I were sitting together at Fraser Street. 'There seems to be so much destruction everywhere. There are wars in the Middle East, Afghanistan, Central America and Southern Africa. Rain forests are being cut down all over the world, elephants are being slaughtered for ivory and that's just a part of it. What can we do?'

'Every disaster, anywhere in the world, should become a reason for you all to meet and discuss how to act swiftly and spontaneously.' His words were very clear. 'The quicker you act, the more divine intervention comes into play. For every one act of cruelty there are a hundred thousand acts of love available, Manu. The only way to counteract the destruction is to create still more powerful ways of loving, resolving, caring and harmonising. Start discovering the multitude of ways to give and to empower the opening of Life's heart.'

Dad was excited, I could tell. 'What do you suggest ?' I asked.

'The signs are all there, Manu. It's time for you to start walking.' It had always been Dad's dream that we would walk around the world for peace, following Gandhi's example of connecting with the ordinary people, sharing love, inspiration and hope wherever he went. I felt suddenly very happy inside that I was going to be instrumental in bringing his dream alive and grateful to the Great Spirit of Life that was guiding me to make it possible. So many things had been happening to show us where our future lay. After we came back from the Nipponzan walk we met a man who was travelling around Europe on foot, talking about the power of walking for peace. We spent many hours talking with him and were very inspired by his words, so I was not surprised by Dad's message to me. We were ready to respond.

'We have all come to earth,' Dad continued, 'to contribute something new and original and to understand or rediscover the original love that lies latent within us individually. When we can use this 'soul force' collectively anything becomes possible.' I could sense that new discoveries awaited us as well as new difficulties and challenges which would give all of us a greater focus for our devotion and strength. Dad reminded me of Gandhi's great words that said, 'I believe that if one man gains spirituality, the whole world gains with him and if one man falls, the whole world falls to that extent. I don't help opponents without at the same time helping myself and my co-workers.'

My father had always urged me to look for ways to create an impact in the world, to create depth in communication and to help people to recognise their potential as spiritual beings.

I felt excited and couldn't wait to tell John. I could already feel the power and energy that rises up inside you when you are pointing yourself in the direction you are meant to go in. You can really feel the universe right there behind you saying 'Yes!'

We had all come so far in only ten short years and so much had happened. Maristowe House was now complete and open as a spiritual focus and centre for healing. We were all teaching yoga in Wales and the Midlands and our family was beginning to grow steadily as many seekers were being drawn to experience the energy that had been created. It was time to open ourselves even more and to take our spirituality out into the world.

Jane had just given birth to our first son and now we were witnessing another birth, the birth of a new era in which we would be walking for peace.

1985 Life Peace Walk

Sometimes when someone speaks to you it's like hearing an echo from your own soul and when Mansukh told me Dad's idea of walking for peace I felt it was one such time.

There was no doubt that the time was right. All we had to do was to step out and trust, knowing that a work of power and beauty would unfold. But as the days went by I also knew that there was something I had to do first.

It was now fourteen years since I had embraced my father for the last time on that bleak mountainside. I knew I had to go back to the place that had changed my life so dramatically because I needed to thank my father, the mountain and destiny for all they had given me. There was no sense of pain or foreboding in my heart, only a deep feeling of gratitude. Looking back over the years I could see more clearly than ever the power of that experience and how it had opened up a part of me that was really in touch with the heartbeat of life. A part of me that was close to God.

When I told Mansukh, he immediately understood and encouraged me to follow my intuition.

'Why don't you ask Glynn to go, too?' he suggested. 'I think that he'd enjoy being with you.'

Glynn, my younger brother, had been only eight when my father died. I knew that to go back to Ben Nevis would be an important journey for him to make as well. He was wonderful company and as we talked on the drive northwards I was really glad that we were going to share such a significant part of our lives after so many years.

It was especially mild for the time of year and on the morning we set out, there was hardly a cloud in the sky. The Glen was at its magical best. The River Nevis sparkled and glistened as it sped over its pebbly bed. Crossing the little footbridge, I was surprised how clearly I remembered the scene. We climbed steadily through the morning, aware that the days were still short, only stopping briefly to savour the views.

It was mid-afternoon by the time we reached the spot where I had found my father. I recognised the bend in the path where the young woman had run to catch up with me. Glynn and I cleared a little patch of ground by the path and I lit a candle and placed flowers on the stony, barren earth. We both sat quietly for a few minutes. I filled the moment with as much love as I could find in myself and, momentarily, I sensed a deep stillness that seemed to settle around us. Something was complete. A chapter had come to a close and now a new one could begin.

Fourteen years earlier I had begun a journey from that barren mountainside. It was a journey that had started in the darkness of despair and grief but as the light of dawn came, it turned into a journey more beautiful than I could ever have imagined. I looked at the tiny, flickering flame and wondered what lay ahead. One thing I was sure of was that greater adventures awaited me as long as I could remain true to my highest purpose.

The authors in Bosnia - Eurowalk 2000

John & Mansukh

Afterword

Now that you have witnessed the power that was moving through the lives of people just like you, please believe that you have the same opportunity to take a leap into the infinity of life with so much trust and faith that nothing is impossible. This true story of a beautiful encounter with God has come to you so that you too can travel further towards your highest goal. Please spread your wings and believe in the power of your own ability to fly.

It is our deepest wish that the words in this book do not harm or hurt you in any way. We hope that they will strengthen your commitment to the path you have already chosen to go on. Please discard whatever is inappropriate for your present situation, keeping it somewhere in the corner of your heart.

May you play, sing, laugh and dance your way through your life, living it to the fullest and may you be content. We leave you with the words of the great Mahatma Gandhi that echo our own deepest feelings towards the rise of the human spirit over the troubles and strife of our modern day life.

> *'I have not the shadow of a doubt that any man or woman can achieve what I have, if he or she would make the same effort and cultivate the same hope and faith.'*

Pathways Index

These Pathways are about a one percent change that makes a one hundred percent difference. We have found that they really work for us, but it is important to recognise that they will only work for you if you want them to. Once you know what you want to achieve, be clear what it will do for you and believe you will succeed when you take it up. Put these exercises into practice, be persistent and they will gently filter through and transform you.

Extra Help

***Body Heart Mind Technology** - a tool box for successful living*
Over the years we have accumulated hundreds of self-help techniques
and skills for healing and strengthening the body, heart and mind. We
call it Body Heart Mind Technology. A few examples from our extensive
range of tapes, books and videos are listed below.

***The Dance between Joy and Pain** -* best-selling book
 by **Dr Mansukh Patel and Rita Goswami**
 This pocket handbook gives you hundreds of simple techniques for
 transforming emotional pain into triumph. Turn hatred to love,
 sadness to joy, loneliness to unity. By working with these and many
 other qualities, you will be empowered to harness the phenomenal
 power of emotions to work for you rather than against you.

***Opening to Miracles** -* tape by **Jane Patel and Sally Langford**
 Five steps to self empowerment and self esteem - These unique
 songs and musical affirmations empower the very highest within you.
 They are also inspirational songs that will set your heart on fire.

***Quiet Times** -* tape by **Chris Barrington**
 This beautiful tape conveys the key principles for successful
 meditation, starting with posture, body awareness, correct breathing
 and awareful relaxation.

***Immortality Sequence** -* tape by **Rita Goswami**
 Rita takes you through this ancient affirmation and mudra sequence
 to an actual experience of your unlimited potential; an experience
 of oneness.

***Back Pain Relief** -* three tapes by **Annie Jones and Paulette Agnew**
 These safe and gentle exercises relieve aches and stiffness in the
 whole of your back, bringing new freedom and energy.

Believe in Yourself - the best-selling tape by **Dr Mansukh Patel**
Here are highly practical ways for building a strong self esteem, and a five-minute technique for transforming negative patterns.

Deep Relaxation - tape by **Anita Goswami**
Lie back and recharge while you release fears, soothe the mind and ease the day's tensions. Please don't use this tape while driving!

Prithvi Namaskara - The Salute to the Earth
tape by **Dr. Mansukh Patel and Annie Jones**
Flowing movements that dissolve feelings of anxiety, panic and stress, bringing calmness and peace with yourself and others.

Ram/Shakti/Krishna - tapes by **John Jones and the Life Team**
Ancient chants and songs that remove fear and facilitate free, heart-felt expression.

Stress Management - tape by **Dr Helena Waters and Anita Goswami**
Simple, quick and effective movement, breathing and relaxation skills that enable you to live a busy life without getting stressed.

For Further Assistance...
Many other products are available to help with a wide range of personal issues, including relaxation, complementary health techniques, stress management, self empowerment, self awareness as well as health, fitness and vitality.

Please send for our full catalogue of tapes, books and videos to:

Life Foundation School of Therapeutics (UK),
Maristowe House, Dover Street,
Bilston, West Midlands WV14 6AL, UK.
Tel +44-(0)1902 409164, Fax +497362

About the Authors

Chasing John and Mansukh around with a tape recorder has been an extraordinary experience for us. Because their lives are so full, it has taken a high degree of skill on our part to pin them down long enough to extract the wealth and beauty contained in this book. We have had to catch them in between their extensive Eurowalk and teaching schedule as, during the compilation of this book, they were touring former Yugoslavia, taking the wisdom they have learned to people who so badly need it. They have taught seminars to aid workers and refugees alike and visited as many people as they could who are trying to rebuild their lives after the war. It has been a very moving experience for us to touch the lives of two people who are so deeply committed to what they believe in.

John is a man with a golden heart. He has a way of completely disarming you with his kindness and gentle manner to such an extent that you are not obviously aware that you are with someone who has great personal power. He speaks softly, but always with a strength and certainty that conveys the sense of purpose he has in his life. In his company you can't help but feel that here is a man who really knows where he is going and has no doubt that he will get there. Many times in talking about the early days of Life he has had us either roaring with laughter or crying with the poignancy of his story.

A man with a mission, Mansukh is always on the move. In fact he never stops teaching and inspiring others to reach their highest potential. Watching him in action you find yourself wondering where he gets the energy to give himself so completely to every situation. He has the ability to love people with a warmth and depth that are very rare and his charisma is such that everyone he meets is instantly changed by their encounter with him. His time in Kenya has provided him with a deep compassion for humanity and he has combined his knowledge as a biochemist and his work with cancer patients to bring emotional, spiritual and physical relief to thousands of people.

We are very grateful for the opportunity to get behind the lives of two such special people who live by their truth and put action behind their vision.

Sally Langford and Andrew Wells
Compilers

What are they all doing now?

Before his death in 1992, Mansukh's father saw the fulfilment of his dream for a World Peace walk when John and Rita led the Friendship Without Frontiers journey which took them to thirty one countries and spanned eighteen months. The title described their mission and objective; to promote friendship between people of every race, colour and creed by discovering what is common to us all.

John teaches Vipassana meditation and Dru Yoga wherever he goes and also has a deep interest in complementary therapies focusing especially on homoeopathy. When at home in North Wales he is the main co-ordinator for all the Life Foundation's building projects.

Rita is an accomplished teacher of Vedanta, the Gita, Dru Yoga and the art of living joyfully. She constantly travels around Britain and abroad sharing her knowledge and regularly supports Thakor in India. Since training as a nurse she has developed programmes for doctors and health professionals building bridges between orthodox and complementary medicine.

Thakor leads the Life Foundation in India and is organising the building of a centre in Moldhara near Navsari. Most of his work is geared towards helping the community, be it towards personal transformation or the education of school children. He also leads peace walks, raising the consciousness of the community as well as being involved in many agricultural projects.

Since Mansukh started the first Life walk in 1985, he has continued to travel extensively, making links with those who are seeking truth. As part of the Eurowalk 2000 team he has travelled across Europe from Auschwitz to Wales, Ireland North and South and more recently from Bosnia to Wales. He is an outstanding speaker and versatile exponent of Vedanta whose vision works constantly towards world peace.

Jane and Mansukh now have three beautiful children and live in North Wales. Jane is well known for her unlimited creativity and is the Life Foundation's musical director and artistic advisor. An expert in Dru Yoga and movement therapy she also leads sound therapy workshops as well as producing many beautiful song tapes. She is a constant support to Mansukh's work and vision and an inspiration to us all.

Annie is as effervescent as ever and an expert in Dru Yoga. She appears on Welsh radio and TV and is the main publicity officer for the Life Foundation. She is also the leading exponent of Body Heart Mind Technology and has extensively toured Britain and America teaching her unique approach to self esteem and successful living. She is well known and loved for her irrepressible joy and ability to make others happy.

Chris has a great depth of knowledge and is highly respected in the field of Dru Yoga, Pranayama and Vipassana meditation. He leads meditation and yoga retreats in the Midlands and North Wales and co-ordinates the Dru Yoga Diploma course in the Midlands. He is an accomplished musician with a special interest in Indian classical music. He also teaches sound therapy.

In Gratitude

We would like to thank the many wonderful people who, through their love and commitment, have catalysed some extraordinary changes during the growth and development of the Life Foundation. To those who have moved on to follow their own paths and dreams, it must be said that the work they have left behind them is unforgettable and indelible. We are very grateful for the extraordinary depth of their contribution to our lives and they will always hold a very special place in our hearts.

Acknowledgements

Our special thanks to Sally Langford for her great contribution in compiling and researching and for making this book possible. Also to Andrew Wells for his patience, understanding and commitment in page setting over many months. To Regina Doerstel for her cover design and artistic advice and Jeff Cushing for the cover photograph and help with graphics. We are grateful to Philip Engelen and Chris Ion for their photographs, and our thanks to Jane Patel, Jean Marvin, Kate Couldwell, Ann Douglas, Jessica Scard and Keith Boaler for their help and suggestions. To Gordon Turner for his one-pointed dedication to the cause of peace and for his photos.

The beautiful translation of the Bhagavad Gita in Part Four is reprinted with permission from 'Gandhi the Man' by Eknath Easwaran, © 1978 Nilgiri Press, Tomales, Ca 94971, USA.
The poem from 'Gitanjali' by Rabindranath Tagore is reprinted with kind permission of Macmillan House Publishers, London.
The Masai picture in Part Two is used with permission of the Koninklijk Instituut Voor De Tropen, Amsterdam.
The picture of the 1985 Life Peace Walk is reproduced with permission of South Wales Argus newspapers.

Day after day, O Lord of my life,
    shall I stand before thee face to face.

With folded hands, O lord of all worlds,
    shall I stand before thee face to face.

Under thy great sky in solitude and silence,
    with humble heart shall I stand before thee face to face.

In this laborious world of thine, tumultuous with
    toil and with struggle, among hurrying crowds shall
    I stand before thee face to face.

And when my work shall be done in this world,
    O King of Kings, alone and speechless
    shall I stand before thee face to face.

                              Rabindranath Tagore

Other Books by
Dr Mansukh Patel

The Peace Formula

Come with Me

The Inside Story

The Dance between Joy and Pain
co-author Rita Goswami

Crisis and the Miracle of Love
co-author Dr Helena Waters

Walking with the Bhagavad Gita
co-authors John Jones & Savitri

Audio Tapes by
Dr Mansukh Patel

Believe in Yourself

Overcome Emotional Pain

Harmonious Relationships

To Listen is to Love

Healing Difficult Relationships

Take Time to Love

The Law of Abundant Energy

Twelve Principles of Transformation

Effective Time & Energy Management

Six Steps to Making Successful Decisions

Meditations for Successful Relationships

Meditations for Inner Strength

Meditations for Dissolving Anger